INVESTORS in PEOPLE Explained

FOURTH EDITION

Peter Taylor & Bob Thackwray

INVESTORS IN PEOPLE

KOGAN PAGE

First published in 1995
Second edition 1996
Third edition 1999
Fourth edition 2001

Kogan Page Limited
120 Pentonville Road
London
N1 9JN
UK

Stylus Publishing Inc.
22883 Quicksilver Drive
Sterling
VA 20166-2012
USA

For further information regarding Investors in People, please contact your local Learning and Skills Council in England and Wales, Local Enterprise Company (LEC) in Scotland or the Training and Employment Agency in Northern Ireland. Alternatively write to Investors in People UK, 7–10 Chandos Street, London W1G 9DQ.

British Library Cataloguing in Publication Data

A CIP record for this book is available from the British Library.

ISBN 0 7494 3460 0

Typeset by JS Typesetting, Wellingborough, Northants
Printed and bound in Great Britain by Clays Ltd, St Ives plc

Contents

Foreword

It is now almost universally understood by employers that people are key to the success of organizations. There is now also a growing consensus around the need to ensure that people have the awareness, ability and motivation to deliver what their organization needs of them.

The Investors in People Standard, launched in 1991, has played a major role in raising awareness and understanding of these issues. Perhaps more importantly, it has provided a practical solution to guide those employers who not only recognize the importance of their people, but who are committed to investing in them actively. It has also given them a mechanism for determining how effective and how valuable that investment has been.

It is often true that more people will sign up to a principle than will commit to activity in support of it. But the staggering success of the Investors in People Standard shows that support for this approach is genuine and is growing all the time.

At the time of writing, over 21,000 organizations have been assessed and formally recognized as meeting the Investors in People Standard. The smallest of these organizations employs only two people, the largest has over 100,000. Investors in People are found in every sector of the economy, from agriculture, mining and manufacturing to schools, colleges and voluntary bodies.

In addition to the 21,000 that have achieved the Standard, another 15,000 organizations are actively involved in working towards Investors in People recognition. In total, over 5 million people (22 per cent of the UK workforce) are employed by organizations which are involved with Investors in People.

Part of the reason for this success must be that Investors in People is based on principles which are proven to work. At the heart of the Standard is the commitment of the organization to continuously improve through good management of its people.

Continuous improvement is also an important feature of the way in which the Standard is applied and delivered. The processes of assessment and recognition, as well as the detail of the Standard itself, are under constant review to ensure that they are clear and relevant, adding value to organizations everywhere.

Ruth Spellman
Chief Executive, Investors in People UK

Acknowledgements

The authors gratefully acknowledge the contributions made by a large number of organizations and individuals, especially: Lesley Bailey, HPC Industrial Products; Dawn Clarke, formerly of West London TEC; Duncan Collins, The Hambledon Group; Bob Cooper and Rodney Godber, Powerminster Limited; Roy Glentworth, Ronseal Limited; Ann Hannon, Barnsley Magistrates' Court; Eamonn Harris, John Marincowicz and Colin Price, Queen Elizabeth's Boys School; Brian Hillier, The Assessment Network; The Industrial Society; Paul Keen, Employment Services (formerly with the Employment Department and ex-acting Chief Executive of Investors in People UK); Lesley Meacham, Jerry Meek, The Royce Consultancy; Barbara Neale, Soluna Travel; Mike Peart, Mike Peart Associates (MPA) and formerly of the Employment Department; Alex Pettifer, Facilities Director, Sheffield Hallam University; Lesley Pritt, Excelsior Hotel; Leslie Rae, Elrae Associates; Fiona Selalmas, formerly of The Royce Consultancy; Ruth Spellman, Chief Executive, Investors in People UK; Bill Sutherland, Strathclyde University; Sue Webb, National Assessor with Investors in People UK; Jan Willoughby, Amwell View School; Joke van Wijk, Director of Human Talent, BIKKER Communicatie BV; Roger van Winkel and Walter van den Elsen, Persyst Consultancy, The Netherlands.

Introduction

The first two editions of this book began with the following quote from Sir Brian Wolfson, past Chairman of the National Training Task Force (NTTF), and Chairman of Wembley plc: 'Investment in equipment depreciates whilst investment in people appreciates', as a 'soundbite' that captures the theme of this book. The third edition added: 'Any company not taking up the Standard needs its collective head examining.' (Michael Parkinson OBE, Chairman, Airedale Springs, Haworth, West Yorkshire). Given the substantial revisions to the criteria within the Investors in People Standard, perhaps an apposite quote for this, the fourth edition would be: '*tempora mutantur nos et mutamur in illis*': times change and we change with them. (John Owen, d.1622).

Since it was first developed and launched in 1990, the Investors in People Standard and its associated processes have undergone a number of changes. This fourth edition brings readers up to date with the many developments and changes made since around the start of 2000.

When this edition was written, towards the end of 2000, many thousands of organizations of all sizes and from all sectors were continuing to recognize that their most important asset is people. Not to take every possible measure to ensure that all employees contribute fully is bad business. Far too high a percentage of companies that run into difficulties or actually cease to exist cite lack of investment in training or employee development as a major contributory factor.

The Investors in People Standard is a mechanism that can provide a framework to support organizations in working out for themselves exactly what is needed, how to go about making it happen and how to evaluate the effectiveness of what has been done. This need not be a complicated process: all it requires is commitment and a certain degree of courage. Commitment because the process once started should be continuous: evaluation is not the last thing you do, it occurs throughout every stage of organizational development. After all, what is evaluation if it is not the turning of hindsight into management information? Courage because the process is one of empowerment and enabling, bringing personal and professional development to its rightful place at the heart of strategic planning.

Over the past twenty years it has become increasingly obvious that the skills and knowledge of people are vital to individual, team and organizational success – in all senses of the word 'success', not just financial. Employers may well have similar levels of access to the same equipment and materials and yet some organizations are evidently much more successful than others. One of the main reasons for this is that they invest more in their people and like any good investment it pays off. It is often the case that this improvement in the quality of the contribution of all employees makes the difference between success and failure.

Investors in People is accepted as one of the major instruments concerned with helping organizations to address these issues. In March 1996, there were 3,514 organizations recognized as Investors in People. By the end of March 1999 that figure had risen to 13,748 with a further 21,701 committed and working towards recognition. Almost a year and a half later those figures had risen to 22,385 recognitions and 21,161 commitments. Therefore, at the end of 2000 54.61 per cent of all UK organizations were committed or recognized.

This book is designed to be of use and interest to a wide variety of organizations and individuals, and to students, managers, trainers, developers and consultants alike, giving a picture of the route to and through the process and incorporating the reflections of various types and sizes of organizations. It seeks to strip away the jargon and to provide the reader with a straightforward and informed account of the origin, development and impact of the Investors in People initiative.

If you or your organization wants to know more about the Standard, or if you are at any stage in the process ranging from thinking about it to heading for re-recognition, this book can provide some answers and, indeed, pose a few more questions! If you are preparing for re-recognition, helpful advice can be found in *Investors in People – Maintained* (2001) or for more practical guidance see *Managing for Investors in People* (2001) (both by the authors of this book).

The book has been designed in four parts. Part One looks at the nature of Investors in People; Part Two explains the Investors in People Standard, principles and indicators in a simple practical way. Part Three describes the experiences of organizations of the various stages in the process; Part Four looks at the way forward.

Intended as a working document, this book can be read from beginning to end or particular sections can be dipped into. All sections and chapters can therefore be read independently of the rest: they are stand-alone accounts of a particular element of the process.

Part One: The Process

Chapter 1 covers the origins and development of Investors in People – who was involved, its launch, what it set out to achieve and why.

In Chapter 2 we answer the question: 'What is Investors in People?' We explain how the concept fits with managing change and supporting business development; how it links to total quality and the concept of continuous improvement. Of particular importance here is the point that it should not be seen as an additional task but that it can be integrated into business processes. Chapter 12 examines in detail how Investors in People links to the concept of a learning organization.

In Chapter 3 we outline in general terms what organizations that have already been recognized as Investors in People say they have gained from the process. As well as covering the added value from the corporate point of view we look at what is in it for individuals.

Chapter 4 should be of interest to all. It explains how Investors in People actually works. It covers how to get started on the journey towards Investors in People status (which many say is more important than the destination) by addressing such key questions as:

- Where am I now?
- What about the things I am already doing or am planning to do?
- How should I involve people?
- What needs to be done?
- Who should do it?
- How long will it take?
- What will it cost?

Chapter 4 also tries to dispel some of the myths that have grown up about Investors in People such as worries about bureaucracy and whether it is just a 'flavour of the month' initiative.

Chapter 5 sets the organization and the role of the assessor in context. It looks at what 'evidence' is and how best to prepare for assessment. It also gives some tips on presenting the case to the assessor. Using our experience of the assessment process, we describe what the process entails and what an assessor's role is, giving some insight into the methodology of the assessment process and some frequently asked questions.

Chapter 6 follows on from assessment through the initial, or first, recognition process and describes the current, changed, role of Recognition Panels. It also looks at what recognition now means and how long it remains in force.

Finally in this section, Chapter 7 looks at particular challenges facing large and multi-site organizations.

Part Two: The Indicators Explained

Chapter 8 starts looking at what lies behind the indicators and evidence requirements, their purpose and what an assessor may look for from the organization.

Chapter 9 continues to examine the indicators and evidence requirements, paying particular attention to those involving the line manager. Line managers are key players in the Investors in People process, and the nature of their involvement is of crucial importance to the success of the venture.

Chapter 10 concludes the examination of the indicators by examining the acid test – those indicators concerning the views of the people themselves.

Part Three: The Experiences

Part Three looks at what it was like for some organizations that have already become Investors in People or are on the journey. Here you will find a number of case studies that reveal the highs and lows of the journey and what the organizations gained from the experience. The organizations selected were chosen for reasons of size, type and nature of activity and the variety of experience they collectively offered.

The organizations included as case studies are:

I.   Amwell View School.
II.   Barnsley Magistrates' Court.
III.   Le Meridien Excelsior Hotel Heathrow.
IV.   HPC Industrial Products Ltd.
V.   Powerminster Limited.
VI.   Queen Elizabeth's Boys School.
VII.   Ronseal Limited.
VIII.   The Royce Consultancy.
IX.   Facilities Directorate, Sheffield Hallam University.
X.   Soluna Travel.
XI.   The University of Strathclyde.
XII.   BIKKER Communicatie BV.

Part Four: Next Steps

To plateau or not to plateau? Things have a habit of going a little cold after an important event such as achieving recognition. Chapter 11 looks at this issue and makes some recommendations set in the context of a number of changes within the Investors in People process itself. In addition, current issues concerning the reassessment process are explored. (This chapter serves as an introduction to *Investors in People – Maintained* (2001) by the same authors.)

Chapter 12 takes the process to the next stage, pulling together some of the key issues and setting the Investors process in the context of the learning organization.

Chapter 13 gives some information about sources of help, including project management software, for those who would like to pursue Investors in People further. It explains the roles of the various organizations to use as sources of help and information and the contributions they can be expected to make. It also outlines the role of consultants in the Investors in People process.

Finally, there are five appendices. The first one gives the full National Standard and the 12 current indicators plus the 33 evidence requirements. The second and third are Investors in People Managers' Surveys; one for senior managers and one for managers. The fourth is an Investors in People Employees' Survey, the fifth shows the Investors in People UK Sample Size Guidelines.

CHAPTER I

Origins and Development

This chapter explores how Investors in People has evolved since its beginnings in 1989. It also examines the roles of people and organizations involved in the various stages of its development. This chapter will be of particular interest and value to students, teachers and trainers and to all those with a general interest in the background and development of Investors in People. Here, by looking at how the Investors in People initiative developed and at the people and organizations involved, we seek to answer the often-asked questions, 'How was it developed?' and 'Where did it come from?'

The beginning

The Investors in People process arose out of repeated reports that demonstrated that, compared to our competitors, Britain's existing workforce held fewer qualifications. One report, *Training in Britain 1987*, published by the Training Agency of the Department of Employment, drew attention to the fact that although £18 billion per annum was spent on training, employers in Great Britain did not spend as much as their competitors and the skills gap was widening. Clearly, something needed to be done.

The stakeholders

The key players in the development of Investors in People were:

- the National Training Task Force (NTTF);
- the CBI;
- the Department of Employment.

The National Training Task Force (NTTF)

The NTTF was set up by the Department of Employment as a result of the 1988 Government White Paper *Employment for the 1990s*. As well as setting the NTTF the task of establishing a network of Training and Enterprise Councils (TECs) it also gave it the remit to 'promote to employers the necessity of their investing in the skills of the working population'. The then Chairman of the NTTF, Sir Brian Wolfson, Chairman of Wembley plc, set up a sub-group to examine how this might be achieved. The sub-group included members of the NTTF, some of the chairmen of the first TECs, and representatives from other interested parties such as the Trades Union Congress (TUC), CBI, and the Association of British Chambers of Commerce, Wales and Scotland.

The CBI

While this activity was taking place the CBI had also established a task force, led by Sir Bryan Nicholson, to look at similar issues. Their report, *Towards a Skills Revolution*, came up with the concept of an Investor in Training, based on 10 principles.

We present those principles (see Figure 1.1) as indicative of the thinking behind the development of Investors in People and because a considerable degree of consistency is evident as the process matures.

These principles and the conclusions reached by the CBI Task Force were very similar to those reached by the NTTF. Comparing the principles in Figure 1.1 with the Investors in People Standard will show just how influential they were in subsequent developments.

The report also set a number of targets. One of the most significant was that 'by 1995 at least half of all medium-sized and larger companies should qualify as "Investors in Training" as

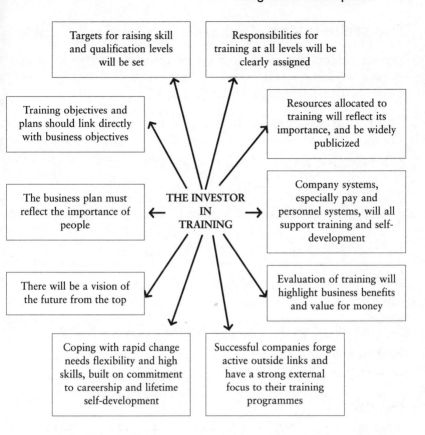

Figure 1.1 *The 10 principles of an Investor in Training*

assessed by the relevant Training and Enterprise Council'. This target would later be amended, replacing 'Investors in Training' with 'Investors in People', after a considerable amount of research about naming the initiative. The targets would also be revised in 1998 as follows: 45 per cent of medium-sized or large organizations and 10,000 small organizations were to be recognized as Investors in People. To achieve these revised targets by 2002, 70 per cent of organizations with 200 plus employees should have been recognized by the end of 2000. By March 2000 54 per cent of organizations in this target group had been recognized.

The White Paper was launched at the CBI Conference in Harrogate in November 1989. At the conference, Norman Fowler, then Secretary of State for Employment, responded to the CBI paper by proposing that the NTTF work with the CBI and with other business and training organizations, including TECs, to develop an 'action programme'.

The Department of Employment

This sub-group commissioned officials from the Department of Employment to consider what employers would have to do to invest in their people. The Department had developed a number of initiatives throughout the 1980s and undoubtedly the research that preceded those initiatives and their subsequent evaluation influenced the ideas produced. Also, in late 1989, a small team was established at the Department's Sheffield headquarters to coordinate this activity. The outcomes were presented to the NTTF and the findings were reported to the Secretary of State.

Action and growth: the emergence of the Standard

Following the conference a working group of practitioners was established who would work to develop the idea of the 'action programme'. The group of practitioners included representatives from a number of government departments, TEC chief executives, CBI, Institute of Personnel Management (IPM), Institute of Training and Development (ITD), TUC, National Council for Vocational Qualifications (NCVQ), industry training organizations and the Association of British Chambers of Commerce. The practitioners' remit was to consider and develop proposals and make recommendations to the NTTF sub-group. Over the next six to nine months the action programme concept was moulded and developed. The idea of a standard based on good practice was mooted.

The criteria chosen for this standard were based on best practice of selected employers. No one employer was used as the model. The Investors in People National Standard was drawn up as a result of studying the good practice of a wide range of successful organizations in all sectors of the economy. As already indicated, it was also influenced considerably by the CBI's 10 principles for an Investor in Training. Finally, it also took into account lessons learnt from a variety of the Department of Employment's initiatives with employers, including the National Training Awards and Business Growth Training.

One over-riding principle was that employers should not feel that this initiative involved government officials and ministers telling them how to run their business. It was not and should not be presented as a top–down initiative. Whatever was developed had to allow businesses to meet the criteria in a way that offered clearly perceived and measurable benefits to each individual business.

An outline of the criteria was drawn up and Coopers & Lybrand were commissioned to test out the validity of both the concept and content with a sample of 20 employers. These employers were carefully chosen by the Department of Employment and the consultants to be representative by size, sector, location, etc. The report from this research would also provide case study material of what employers actually did in practice. Research outcomes clearly indicated the need for an assessment framework. This led to PriceWaterhouse being commissioned to develop such a framework.

From July 1990 some of the early TECs and the then residual Area Offices of the Training Agency and the Office for Scotland were invited to pilot the concept with employers in their areas. These pilots were the first stage in selling the potential benefits of the initiative to the people who would eventually have to run with it. The pilots met with mixed levels of success but in general confirmed significant interest levels among employers.

Where did the name Investors in People come from?

While the pilots were progressing, market research was being undertaken to establish the name. Makrotest (now CEGOS Makrotest) carried out the research throughout June and July 1990. A number of key words and slogans were brainstormed and tested out, using a mixture of telephone research and group discussion, with a sample of 500 business people and associated agencies. The outcome was presented to the NTTF sub-group together with a logo that had been designed. Their decision resulted in the current logo and the name Investors in People.

The launch

The name was announced and the Investors in People National Standard launched by Michael Howard, Secretary of State for Employment, at the CBI Conference in Glasgow in November 1990.

PriceWaterhouse, meanwhile, were developing the assessment framework. This work, together with the continuation of the pilots and an invitation to TEC staff to identify companies which they felt to be close to meeting the criteria, culminated in around 40 companies being assessed during the summer of 1991. Of these, 28 met the Standard and were subsequently recognized at a media event held in London on 16 October 1991. In addition to recognizing the first Investors in People the event also provided a summary of progress to date and listed those companies which had made a commitment to work towards the Standard.

For these first assessments the process was overseen by KPMG Peat Marwick, which reported that the assessment framework had proven robust. Adjustments were made to the wording of some of the performance indicators as a result of this exercise, but these were in the main quite minor. Some of the early concerns voiced by employers were about potential bureaucracy and the quality of the assessors. In particular, how could it be ensured that the National Standard would be applied nationally? Throughout the next 18 months quality assurance measures were established to address these issues. The lessons learnt from the first assessments were disseminated to all those who had been involved and to those who were drawn in later.

The twin terrors of bureaucracy and interference still surface today. However, the launch of the current Standard on 13 April 2000 has done much to further allay these fears. The rest is up to organizations themselves (the Standard works for them and not they for it), and to assessor and adviser development. In the following chapters we will demonstrate that such worries are groundless if the organization has, or wishes to have, a culture that sees the benefits of continuous professional development for all its employees.

The demise of the NTTF

When the NTTF was established it was given four years to complete its task and therefore ceased to exist at the end of 1992. The NTTF sub-group had developed a number of roles during the previous 15 months which would create a vacuum if it too was wound up so it was agreed that this group, under the chairmanship of Sir Allen (now Lord) Sheppard, Chairman and Chief Executive Officer of Grand Metropolitan plc, would continue to carry out its role. This role had been widened to cover all aspects of Employer Investment (in the employer's workforce). The enhanced role included:

- overseeing the further development of the initiative;
- recognition of those TECs that had been assessed by National Assessors as having met the criteria;
- recognition of some large and multi-site organizations which had chosen to go as a whole.

In the spring of 1993 a successor body to the NTTF was announced, named the National Advisory Committee for Education and Training Targets (NACETT), and given the remit of encouraging organizations to work towards the National Education and Training Targets. From April 2001 much of the work of NACETT was to be subsumed within the role of the Learning and Skills Council (see Chapter 13).

Establishing Investors in People UK

The sub-group continued to operate until the end of June 1993. On 1 July 1993 a new body, Investors in People UK, was established and chaired by Sir Brian Wolfson. The membership of this body was appointed by the Secretary of State following consultation with the TEC movement.

It was announced that this body would have an executive arm, a private company limited by guarantee, which would take over some of the work that had previously been undertaken by officials in the Department of Employment. A Chief Executive Officer, Mary Chapman, formerly Director of Personnel Operations and

Management Development with the L'Oréal Group in the UK, took up the post on 1 December 1993. The current Chief Executive, Ruth Spellman, took over on 1 October 1998. She was formerly Human Resource Director for the National Society for the Prevention of Cruelty to Children.

The role of Investors in People UK is to:

- be the 'protector' of the Standard;
- market and promote Investors in People nationally;
- provide a national assessment and quality assurance service.

The first stages in taking this role forward were marketing strategies:

1. Launching the company in January 1994.
2. Conferences for Chief Executives of major companies first held in May 1994.
3. 'Investors in People Weeks' during October every year; the first one was in 1994.

Investors in People UK introduced licences for training providers to train assessors.

Investors in People – overseas

Since its early days Investors in People has attracted a great deal of interest from abroad, notably from Australia, where it is now well established. Investors in People UK are working with partners to establish the Standard in 11 other countries – including for example Holland (where Investors in People (NL) went live in January 2000). Other countries involved include Bermuda, Chile, New Zealand, Finland, Germany, Sweden, Malaysia, Jersey, Guernsey and the Isle of Man. In addition, for some time now a project involving multi-national organizations has been running, involving organizations in New Zealand, Germany, France, Spain, Belgium and Switzerland.

Subsequent chapters in this book will outline the process of becoming an Investor in People and the involvement of the TECs and now the Learning and Skills Councils. Arrangements in Scotland and Northern Ireland are slightly different, and the more significant differences are outlined below.

Investors in Scotland

Scotland has Local Enterprise Companies (LECs) instead of TECs/ LSCs. Although LECs carry out the same basic functions, they have an enhanced role as they also carry out the functions of either Scottish Enterprise or Highlands and Islands Enterprise. The decision was taken early in the development of Investors in People to set up a separate company, Investors in People Scotland Ltd, which would carry out assessments on behalf of the LECs. All the work prior to assessment is carried out by the LECs. It is worth noting here that although TECs in England and Wales will be wound up by the end of March 2001, LECs will continue. This model will be examined further in Chapters 6 and 7.

Investors in Northern Ireland

Northern Ireland has neither TECs nor LECs. The Training and Employment Agency (T&EA), an executive agency within the Department of Higher and Further Education, Training and Employment, carries out their role. The Agency's involvement with Investors in People began in early 1993, with the first recognitions of Investors in People in October of that year. The Agency carries out the same role as TECs in England and Wales and will be referred to throughout the following chapters.

The continuous review of the Standard

It was always intended that the Standard should be constantly reviewed to ensure that it remained at the leading edge of human resource development.

The first major review: 1995–96

The first project to review the Standard and make recommendations on its future development took place during 1995. The objectives of the review were to:

- ensure the continued relevance and credibility of Investors in People as a framework for organization improvement and as a benchmark of good practice;

- anticipate future trends in people management and organization development;
- position the Standard accordingly in the wider context of quality management initiatives, standards and awards.

Following consultation and debate, the revisions were agreed early in 1996 and revised indicators were then introduced. All organizations assessed after 31 March 1997 were assessed against the revised indicators.

The actual changes comprised some rewording of individual indicators to provide greater clarity and therefore more consistent interpretation; some indicators were relocated to improve the link between indicators; the evaluation indicators were reordered and overlapping indicators were combined. The Standard itself did not change.

The second major review: 1998–2000

This began with the Strategic Review of Assessment and Recognition (The STAR project), which focused largely on the assessment process. It went through various stages of consultation during 1998 and 1999 and reported back in late 1999.

At the same time another project – the LASER project – began which concerned a review of the Investors in People Standard. The previous review (in 1995) had led to effective, although not major, changes to the content of the Standard. Three years on it was felt to be appropriate to consult stakeholders again. This time the purpose was to agree options for the further development of Investors in People if or where required.

Investors in People UK said that a fundamental premise of the review was that the Standard should exist in the most appropriate format to meet customer needs. In this context customers are defined as UK organizations, both private and public sector, of all sizes and types. Stakeholders, in addition to customers, include the Department for Education and Employment (DfEE), the TEC/LEC network, the T&EA in Northern Ireland, National Training Organisations (NTOs), representative bodies such as the CBI and the TUC, and other government departments.

The LASER project was set up in October 1998 with initial consultation towards the end of that year. By the end of the year stakeholder objectives had been agreed and key issues identified. The national Visioning Group (of which one of the authors of this book was a member) first met in December 1998 and agreed the options for the future development of the Standard. During January and February 1999 consultation on the need to, and options for, change involved 28 regional focus groups. In March 1999 the Visioning Group met for a second time, this time to evaluate the options and advise on an appropriate way forward. These proposals were accepted by the Board of Investors in People UK at the end of March 1999. During the remainder of 1999 the proposed revisions to the Standard were tested by a group of assessors as they carried out assessments. There were further consultations with employers and Investors in People UK partners before a final version of the Standard was launched on 13 April 2000.

Why change the Standard?

Investors in People UK list the following key objectives for undertaking their review of the Standard and implementing the subsequent changes:

- to achieve greater accessibility to a wider audience;
- to provide greater relevance for employers and employees;
- to ensure that the Standard becomes more effective in driving change and continuous improvement;
- to provide greater flexibility to meet the needs of a range of organizations and working styles.

What are the key changes?

- The Standard is now based on outcomes rather than processes.
- The principles have been reworded as outcomes.
- An explicit indicator on equal opportunities has been included.
- There is more emphasis on the underpinning principles and 'spirit' of Investors in People.
- There is clearer language with less jargon, and fewer indicators.
- Key terminology changes include: 'development of people' rather than 'training and development', and the use of the word 'people' rather than 'employees'.

- Indicators have been relocated under the principles to which they logically relate.
- There has been a combining of indicators where appropriate.
- Evidence requirements are now mandatory.
- Indicators are now numbered 1–12 as opposed to 1.1, 1.2 etc.

In addition, the research from the focus groups found that employers sought additional 'stretch' from continuing to work with the Investors in People Standard. With this in mind a number of 'stretch' modules are being developed and one (recruitment and selection) is currently being piloted.

Practitioner development

Whilst the above projects were taking place, so was another – to review the competences of all Investors Practitioners. CMS Consultancy Services was commissioned to consult the Investors in People delivery network about the recruitment and selection, initial training and development, continuing professional development and qualifications of all practitioners. The project led to the development of a new set of competences which were tested during a series of pilots during 1999. These competences were refined and accepted as the Performance Review Framework by the Investors in People UK Board, and are being introduced from April 2001. All new practitioners will need to demonstrate their competence against these criteria before they are allowed to operate. Existing practitioners will need to be reviewed against the competences by September 2001 and any development needs will be identified and a plan to address them drawn up.

In addition, the changes as a result of the STAR and LASER projects clearly led to a number of development needs for Investors Practitioners, particularly for assessors. During the first months of 2000 all assessors and advisers were required to undertake training in the application of the changes to the indicators.

Summary

We have described how Investors in People was created by the work of the CBI, the NTTF and the Department of Employment. This chapter has explored how the process and materials were developed and piloted prior to the formal recognition of the first Investors in People in 1991. It has charted the establishment and development of the national body, Investors in People UK, and highlighted relevant elements of the continuous review of the Standard, the process and the development of the various practitioner roles over a 10-year period.

CHAPTER 2

What is Investors in People?

This chapter is essential reading. It explains what Investors in People is; how it can support business and organizational development; and shows that it should not be viewed as additional work but as an integral part of what ought to be everyday business activity. This is examined in context with other contemporary initiatives such as Total Quality, ISO 9000 and the European Foundation for Quality Model (EFQM) often referred to in the UK as the Business Excellence Model. The chapter also shows how Investors in People can be used effectively in support of the management of change.

The concept

The central focus of Investors in People is the National Standard for Effective Investment in People. This is now more commonly known as the Investors in People Standard (see Figure 2.1).

The concept is deceptively simple. Employing organizations are encouraged to meet the Standard. If they do, they will be recognized (or continue to be recognized) as an Investor in People; if they do not, they will be encouraged to take the required action to meet it or retain it. They are then encouraged (or more appropriately

Principle One: Commitment
An Investor in People is fully committed to developing its people to achieve its aims and objectives.

Principle Two: Planning
An Investor in People is clear about where it wants to be and what its people need to do to get it there.

Principle Three: Action
An Investor in People develops its people effectively in order to improve performance.

Principle Four: Evaluation
An Investor in People understands the impact of its investment in people on its performance.

Figure 2.1 *Investors in People Standard*

they encourage themselves) to maintain and continue to build on this recognition.

As indicated in Chapter 1, the Standard is based on good practice and therefore meeting it makes good business sense. We have yet to find anyone who disagrees with the principles underpinning the Standard. This does not, of course, mean that actually going for recognition as an Investor in People is universally regarded as a good thing. On the contrary, some organizations express strong views as to why they feel it is inappropriate for them.

Development is an investment not a cost

The single most important factor differentiating one company from another is the skills, knowledge and expertise of its people. This is especially true in the increasingly technological world we live in, where people's skills are often the only major resource. Most people have access to similar ranges of equipment, technology and other facilities. Therefore it is how well these facilities are used that makes the difference. The service sector especially relies considerably on the skills and attitudes of people to demonstrate commitment to the efficient delivery of a quality service.

That notwithstanding, research continually demonstrates that many organizations do not consider the learning and development of their people as an investment. They see it as a cost. It is therefore not planned strategically nor is it clearly linked to business objectives. It is not equally available to all employees. It is rarely evaluated at the point of delivery, let alone later in terms of its impact on effectiveness of working practices.

This situation gives rise to many questions, notably: 'How much time and money is wasted?' and 'Do all our people know what they are doing and why?' 'Can something be done to ensure that training and development budgets are spent more effectively?'

What is new or different about Investors in People?

Very little! The Investors in People Standard historically is based on standards of good practice that a wide range of organizations have been employing to greater or lesser degrees for some time, as mentioned in Chapter 1. What is different, therefore, is that examples of good practice taken from this range of organizations have been packaged in a coherent way to deliver a number of outcomes. Consequently, the Standard can offer organizations a framework that has the potential to be used strategically to tackle a range of business issues and their linked training and development activities. This framework is examined in the following chapters. It follows therefore that training and development can and should become integrated into the culture of the organization.

One new feature is the formal recognition. This can be used by an organization to show the outside world what has been achieved. Investors in People status increasingly results in well-trained and better-motivated workforces as several studies have shown, notably that carried out by the Hambleden Group (see Chapter 3).

Most organizations that have started work on becoming Investors in People see the journey as far more important than the actual destination, with the process taking precedence over the 'badge'. This, of course, is entirely within the spirit that created Investors in People in the first place. Although there are legitimate benefits to be gained from being recognized as an Investor in People, the real gain is in going through the process, when there are benefits for all, but it is clear that those organizations furthest away from meeting the Standard will have the most to gain.

Is it 'just another initiative'?

Those who worked on its creation and the majority of recognized organizations would say definitely not. Although organizations that have travelled the Investors in People journey may have started by thinking it was only about training, they all confirm that it has turned out to be much more. Indeed the current standard does not mention training at all. The focus is rightly on development. A large number of organizations have said it has had a major impact on the way they carry out their business. (See the case studies in Part Three; Chapter 3; and later in this chapter.)

The main features of an Investor in People

An organization that is an Investor in People will:

- plan ahead;
- be clear about what it is trying to achieve and continually monitor progress towards its goals;
- be clear what skills and knowledge are needed to achieve these goals and targets, and deliver the plan;
- have identified what skills and knowledge its people already have;
- plan and take action to fill any gaps between the skills and knowledge already held and those needed;
- look back after the action has been taken to see what impact it has had on the business, whether the action was effective in filling the gap, and if it was not, take further action.

All such action will be taken in the context of the needs and direction of the business. As business or organizational needs and directions constantly change and develop, new gaps will be created and further action taken. As there is also a need for organizations to strive for continuous improvement in order to maintain performance, rather like painting the Forth Bridge, the task never ends.

Achieving Investors in People status therefore is merely a milestone on the journey. Retaining the status is the next milestone.

The framework or model

It can be difficult to see how the Standard as illustrated in Figure 2.1 can be described as a framework or model of good practice. It is also not easy to assess an organization against the Standard in that form. The Standard has therefore been broken down into 12 indicators and 33 evidence requirements against which an organization can be assessed. These indicators and evidence requirements are reproduced in Appendix 1. Chapters 8, 9 and 10 explore the meaning and rationale of each one and how they link together. It is, therefore, the indicators and evidence requirements that lead to the framework that can then be used in support of organizations in a variety of situations, as illustrated below.

Developing the business and business development

This heading may appear to suggest that this section is only relevant to private sector organizations. As is now well documented, there is increasing pressure on public and voluntary sector organizations to be more accountable, more efficient and, in some cases, to generate income. Business development may therefore be of particular relevance to them.

From the first organizations to be recognized evidence has emerged that Investors in People has contributed significantly to business performance (see Chapter 3).

Managing change and changing management

All organizations are facing change of some description. Typical corporate changes may include delayering or flattening structures (and in some cases relayering when delayering went too far!), multiskilling or flexible working practices and the introduction or improvement of quality approaches. Change is not now seen as undesirable, of course. As innovation and improvement-oriented management philosophies and methodologies 'bite ever deeper' into the reality of everyday working life, so managed and directed change becomes essential to organizational competitiveness, development and growth. Certainly, the ability to handle change more quickly and more effectively than competitors is a key issue in maintaining business performance.

For some, when facing change, knowing where to start is the most difficult part. To meet the Investors in People Standard, organizations will require a number of frameworks or models that can be used to facilitate the process. For example, the Standard requires a framework by which aims and objectives can be clarified, and become more focused and planned. It also requires models for implementing, monitoring and reviewing progress.

The example changes mentioned above invariably have a major impact on the role of line managers. Delayering leads to having fewer managers; having flexible and/or multi-skilled teams leads to changes in the way staff are managed. Line managers are clearly key players in helping their organization achieve Investors in People status. Managers are increasingly encouraged to act as leaders and to demonstrate this by empowering, supporting, coaching, mentoring and consulting their people. (For a more in-depth examination of the part they can play, see Chapter 9).

Quality

Whether operating in the manufacturing or the service sector, quality of product or service is a critical factor and necessarily sets an organization apart from its competitors. There are so many different approaches to quality improvement and so many books that concentrate on them that this section merely aims to highlight linkages.

A popular approach has been to introduce quality systems, usually opting for ISO 9000 (originally BS 5750). Quality systems generally underpin the approach to quality. They will involve a significant investment and rely on people to adhere to the systems. The changes introduced with the introduction of ISO 9000:2000 have strengthened the linkages and overlaps with Investors in People. ISO 9000:2000 requires top management to demonstrate their commitment to quality. This includes a commitment to ensuring people performing work affecting product quality are provided training and that the organization can demonstrate that they evaluate the effectivensss of the actions taken. Learning and development are therefore central components when introducing ISO 9000:2000, so that they are not only adhered to but also understood. Many organizations feel that if they are introducing quality systems they 'have enough on their plates without introducing Investors in People as well'. If the Investors in People Standard is correctly used as the framework for the introduction of the systems it should not create extra work: it should merely ensure that the learning associated with it follows good practice and is effective.

Investors in People is most certainly not merely about training. A by-product of the simultaneous introduction of Investors in People and quality systems will be that other changes, often cultural, will take place, leading organizations to a further stage in quality improvement, often called Total Quality. A number of organizations and writers on management theory and practice would argue that quality systems plus Investors in People is very close to the concept of Total Quality. Careful examination of the Standard reveals that it is very close to the 'plan, do, check' concept favoured by some Total Quality gurus (or plan, do, check, *act*, as the Management Charter Initiative (MCI) describes it).

Another approach to quality improvement, especially in the service sector, is to have customer service statements; in the public sector often linked to seeking accreditation through a charter mark. Implementing these approaches involves training and development but most of all it should mean a change of culture leading to greater commitment from staff to delivering a quality service and meeting increasingly demanding customer expectations. Using the Investors in People framework can help achieve this.

Organizational development

The changes mentioned above usually lead to the formation of new teams and sometimes to the formation of teams for the first time. Some will be permanent, whereas others will have been brought together to work cross-functionally. Whatever the situation, the members of new teams need to learn to work together and frequently the first steps are to have a number of team-building events. Clarity of purpose is the starting-point for any team-building activity and the Standard, especially those aspects associated with planning and communication, can therefore be used as a model and the remaining parts to implement, control and evaluate the process.

Redundancy

A number of organizations have been recognized as Investors in People while at the same time making people redundant. There are three key considerations in this situation:

- the people who are not being made redundant will probably face different roles when the others have left;
- the remaining people will have training and development needs;
- those who are leaving may need help to secure other jobs.

Therefore the employer's approach to providing back-up can have an effect on those made redundant, on the organization's customers and also on those staying on, who may feel reassured that if further redundancies are necessary they too will be helped. Nevertheless, the point must be made that working for an organization with Investors in People status is not an automatic guarantee of job satisfaction and continuity and it should not be presented as such.

Clearly, when introducing the concept of Investors in People in these situations sensitive handling is essential, with organizational and individual benefits being the main focus.

The concept of a learning organization

The concept of a learning organization developed out of the self-development movement, which began in the 1970s. This movement stressed the need for individuals to take responsibility for addressing their own training and career development needs. In order to enable this to happen organizations need to create the right environment. However, there are many definitions of what actually constitutes a learning organization.

During the last few years interest and debate around the concept has increased. Clearly the issues that have been outlined in this chapter are pertinent to the debate but, for readers who wish to explore them further, more detail is given in Chapter 12.

The EFQM/Business Excellence Model

The European Foundation for Quality Management (EFQM) was formed in 1988. In 1991 it established the European Quality Award (EQA). Britain promptly followed suit, and the British Quality Foundation (BQF) was established in 1993 and created the UK Quality Award in 1994. These Foundations offered businesses an opportunity to demonstrate their commitment to (and achievements in) quality and encouraged them to compete for their awards.

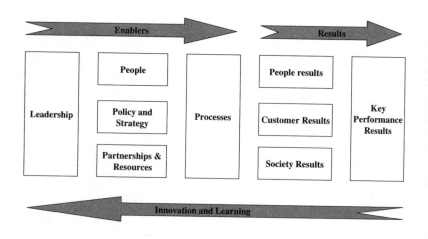

Figure 2.2 *The Excellence Model*

(*Source:* EFQM)

This model offers organizations a framework highlighting a number of key issues to address which should help them improve their overall business performance. The framework consists of a number of enablers such as leadership, people management, processes, etc with criteria designed against acknowledged 'best practice', through to its resultant 'impact on society' and detailed business results (see Figure 2.2). As with any model, the 'good practice' can be used internally to benchmark progress and there are courses available to train internal assessors. There is also an option to bring in external assessors, whether or not the organization decides to enter the competition for the UK Quality Award. Using the model, the assessors will identify whether the organization is able to demonstrate effectiveness of current practice against each section of the model. They may wish to track between three and five years' performance trends to demonstrate continuous improvement. Organizations might also wish to provide evidence of benchmarking of its practices with other businesses that are recognized for excellence. Proponents say the strength of using EFQM for any organization is that it is a framework for continuous improvement and is not limited by the need to reach specific standards.

There is an ongoing dialogue between Investors in People UK and EFQM with the aim of enabling all potential customers of any business improvement to be able to see what is right for them. The authors believe that competition in this instance is inappropriate. It is the needs of organizations and their people that should remain the focus. Business excellence and Investors in People are complementary.

What's in it for individuals?

Most of what has been written in this chapter has focused on the needs of organizations. The Standard is designed to place development of people at the centre of the corporate agenda by linking it to the business planning process. Clearly for most organizations development demands that lie well outside these corporate parameters cannot always be met. Investors in People is not a mandate to provide any or all the development that is requested. That notwithstanding, clear evidence does now exist that shows that pay in recognized organizations has increased significantly more than that in organizations generally (see Chapter 3).

Continuous professional development (CPD)

For those individuals who are members of professional institutions the concept of continuous professional development (CPD) will be familiar. Most, if not all, institutions now demand that to maintain their membership, members must provide evidence of CPD.

This concept sits readily within Investors in People. In this instance the framework can be applied to an individual: plan, take action and evaluate. As well as satisfying individual requirements, the achievement of CPD will also provide evidence for the organization.

Succession planning

It has sometimes been argued that succession planning and development beyond the needs of the immediate job are not catered for in the Investors in People Standard. This is not true. The Standard requires a framework for strategic planning for both the business and the people to deliver the plans. This must include succession planning and the resultant development needs of the people.

Summary

This chapter has attempted to clarify what the Investors in People Standard is and explain how it is not merely about training; that it is not something that is 'bolted on' to other initiatives associated with business development; that it should be an integral part of everyday business activity.

The links to a variety of contemporary business issues have been explored, as have the ways in which the Standard can be used as a framework or model to manage the various issues associated with change and development facing all types of organization in every sector.

CHAPTER 3

Why Bother?

We now examine the question of why organizations, teams and individuals should 'bother'. 'You can't afford not to' is a popular response, and versions of it are used by promoters of Investors in People all over the UK. Is it true? What are the perceived benefits of the process? Does it confer a range of advantages on the company or institution as is claimed? What are the views of those who have gone through the process, those who are going through it and those who do not currently want to? What are the concerns?

Issues for organizations

Regardless of sector there are a number of common issues that face many organizations:

- The difficulties associated with making plans for the future in a turbulent economic – and competitive – environment.
- The continuous need to improve quality, productivity and efficiency (ie doing more with less and making it better).
- The importance of increased flexibility to allow organizations to become more responsive to the needs of customers, clients, etc.
- The growing recognition of the crucial importance of people to organizational success.

These concerns lead to a number of challenges for managers, especially all those with responsibility for managing people:

- How to manage people in a way that will directly contribute to improved performance.
- How to plan and organize the development of people so they are able to contribute to the success of the organization.
- How to gain people's commitment and enthusiasm.
- How to develop people so they become a real source of competitive advantage. (This will be particularly relevant for those in the private sector).

Of course, the question underpinning all of the above is – where to begin?

For some organizations Investors in People has already made a significant contribution to addressing these issues. Recognition of this is demonstrated by the increasing number of organizations working towards achieving Investors in People status.

The latest statistics

Almost ten years after the initiative was launched in October 1991, 22,385 organizations were recognized with a further 21,161 committed. This represents about 39 per cent of the workforce (figures courtesy Investors in People UK). For current figures, you can visit the Investors in People UK Web site: http://www.investors inpeople.co.uk/

Many of those companies who achieved recognition have gone through the process of re-recognition, some a number of times, and most have been re-recognized.

How progress has been made

An IRS survey of employers' experience published in March 1994 demonstrated that after a 'painfully slow start' participation was increasing. At that time only 677 organizations were recognized, although another 5,630 were committed. Interestingly, these figures were to jump considerably even by the end of that month (to 739 recognitions and over 6,300 commitments). Clearly interest was on the up – as our later figures demonstrate – but whose interest? The IRS survey noted that about two-thirds of organizations achieving recognition were small companies (ie they employed fewer than 200 people). Another significant feature coming out of the survey was that over a quarter were organizations whose business was education and training. This is hardly surprising: it is obvious that a national standard for training and development would be much sought after by such organizations, and that they would often be in a position to learn of and react to the Investor in People initiative more quickly than most other organizations.

It might be expected that this trend would at the very least slow down. In 2000 this appeared to be the case. While the number of commitments remained constant for a couple of years, the number of recognitions increased from just under 4,000 at the end of 1996 to well over 22,000. (See Figure 3.1.)

An additional complication in comparing these figures is that the TECs 'clean up' their list of commitments periodically, deleting organizations which have been counted as 'committed' but are not very active in working towards the Standard.

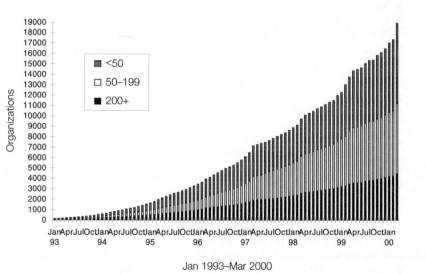

Jan 1993–Mar 2000

Figure 3.1 *Cumulative recognitions*

(*Source:* Investors in People UK)

The expansion of interest in some sectors such as education is impressive. The National Committee of Inquiry into Higher Education, 1997 (the Dearing Report) was one of many significant drivers resulting in many universities and colleges of higher education engaging with the process. It recommended that 'over the next year, all institutions should . . . consider whether to seek the Investors in People award' (Recommendation 47, extract) and found that 'the principles and practices that inform it are sound and relevant.' (See the University of Strathclyde case study on page 156.)

The Labour Government reiterated the previous government's commitment that all government departments and their agencies should be recognized by 2000. (See Figure 3.2).

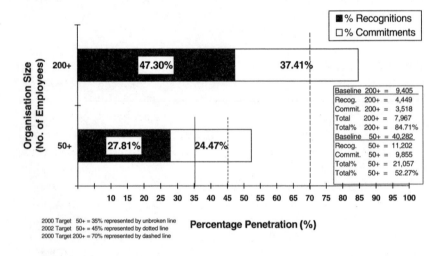

Figure 3.2 *Progress towards achieving national targets*

Source: Investors in People UK website http://www.investorsinpeople.co.uk/

The introduction from 1996–97 of National Training Organizations (NTOs), with achievement of Investors in People as a key objective, is a further example of the embedding of Investors in People (see Chapter 13). During the first three years of the Standard, the ratio of recognized organizations employing fewer than 200 to those employing over 200 was constant at 2:1. As 96 per cent of employers in the UK employ fewer than 20 people, this statistic shows that the ratio of large companies is good. However, concern has been expressed that not enough blue chip companies are coming forward, though it is difficult to be exact about this as large companies are tending to approach Investors in People by piloting in small autonomous units (see Chapter 7). To address this concern, Investors in People UK established a pilot programme with the aim of taking 15 multi-nationals to recognition. Some of the major hurdles encountered by large organizations were the authority and autonomy criteria. These were revised in July 1998, enabling large complex organizations like universities, the Church of England and building societies to move forward on a much more appropriate 'building block' approach. (See Chapter 7 for a full account of the 'building block' approach.)

People *are* bothering – why?

Evidently, the question 'Why bother?' is being answered positively by an increasing number and variety of companies and organizations. Reasons for participation vary but several common themes emerge as evidenced by research carried out on behalf of Investors in People UK in 1996. This survey, of 231 organizations, showed that the following reasons triggered the adoption of the Standard:

- to improve competitive edge (72 per cent);
- to provide a framework for people management (69 per cent);
- to aid business/HR alignment (62 per cent);
- for benchmarking of training and development (58 per cent);
- to enhance corporate image (41 per cent);
- to provide a vehicle for a change programme (32 per cent);
- to give confirmation of good practice (30 per cent).

(Source: *Shaping up for Change through Investors in People*, published by Investors in People UK.)

The actual benefits

The same research showed that the 231 organizations surveyed cited the following benefits as having emerged at the time the research was carried out:

- sharper focus for training and development (62 per cent);
- motivated workforce (59 per cent);
- better customer service (55 per cent);
- effective communication (52 per cent);
- better corporate image (43 per cent);
- better appraisal strategy (36 per cent);
- more skilled workforce (35 per cent);
- higher productivity (30 per cent);
- improved retention (27 per cent);
- increased profitability (26 per cent);
- higher calibre recruits (22 per cent);
- increased turnover (18 per cent);
- reduced stock levels (18 per cent);
- reduced training costs (13 per cent).

An examination of the case study companies in Part Three also shows that many of the above, and other, benefits have emerged as follows:

- improved performance (Amwell View School; Barnsley Magistrates' Court; Le Meridien Excelsior Hotel; Powerminster; Queen Elizabeth's Boys School; The Royce Consultancy; Sheffield Hallam University Facilities Directorate; Soluna Travel);
- external recognition of improvement (for example, by Ofsted: Amwell View School, Queen Elizabeth's Boys School; National training awards: Le Meridien Excelsior Hotel, Queen Elizabeth's Boys School);
- forming 'the umbrella that brought everything together' (Ronseal Limited);
- improved or more robust systems and increased clarity (Amwell View School; HPC; Soluna Travel; University of Strathclyde);
- improved staff morale, increased commitment, more willingness to get involved (Barnsley Magistrates' Court; HPC; The Royce Consultancy; Soluna Travel);
- reduced staff turnover (Le Meridien Excelsior Hotel);
- improved survival prospects (Barnsley Magistrates' Court).

Investors in People UK case studies show that the 60 recognized organizations it surveyed in 1995 are quoting the following benefits to which Investors in People has contributed:

- increased profitability (Boots the Chemist; De Vere Hotels; ICL);
- increased efficiency (Hydro Polymers; IBS);
- increased sales and income (Bettys and Taylors of Harrogate; Land Rover; Lawdon Mardon Plastics);
- reduced costs (Brooke Bond Foods, Worksop; IDV UK, Essex).

The Hambleden Group (1998) produced a report for Investors in People UK that compares recognized organizations with those that are not involved in the process. (See Table 3.1).

Table 3.1 *Recognized organizations*

Return on sales	192%	Higher than the median
Return on capital employed	97%	Higher than the median
Return on assets managed	41%	Higher than the median
Average remuneration	19%	Higher than the median
Turnover per employee	106%	Higher than the median
Profit per employee	734%	Higher than the median
Return on human capital	700%[1]	Higher than the median

Source: The Hambleden Group 1998

As part of recent research, *Building Capability for the 21st Century* (CREATE 1999), 2000 recognized organizations were polled. This research confirmed previous research, finding that through involvement in Investors in People:

- 70 per cent had increased competitiveness;
- 70 per cent had increased productivity;
- 80 per cent had increased customer satisfaction.

A number of organizations have also referred to Investors in People as stimulating continuous improvement initiatives. Others talk of improved management skills. There are also benefits for individuals such as improved opportunities for skill and career development, and access to qualifications. Individuals have also referred to managers managing more effectively which led to increased involvement, support, encouragement and recognition. The overriding message is:

improved communication = better informed people = increased commitment.

So the key message has been consistent: working towards the good practice inherent in the Investors in People Standard pays off – frequently directly on the bottom line!

Evaluating the benefits

Interestingly, 13 per cent of the 231 organizations surveyed found that they benefited through *reduced* training costs, which appears to have been achieved through raising the efficiency of training budgets. This links to the benefit of sharper focus for training and development, which is often achieved through better planning and improved evaluation of training. This is an area where Investors in People has a great effect, as shown by the results of the following survey.

In 1994 the Industrial Society reported the results of the Managing Best Practice Survey of 457 personnel and training professionals. (The authors are grateful to the Society for permission to reproduce some of their findings.) The aim of the survey was to produce a current picture of the evaluation of training across a wide spectrum of organizational types. The topics covered included:

- responsibility for evaluation;
- commitment to evaluation;
- why there is the trend for evaluation;
- evaluation methods;
- training and development areas evaluated;
- measuring effects of evaluation;
- obstacles to evaluation;
- benefits from evaluation.

Most organizations employ someone whose responsibilities include the evaluation of training and development, but 19 per cent of organizations surveyed carried out no systematic evaluation of training and development (see Figure 3.3).

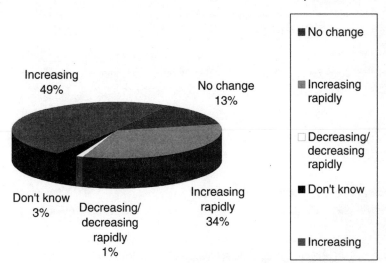

Figure 3.3 *Organizations' commitment to training evalation over the next two years*

(Source: Industrial Society, 1994*)*

The survey also confirms that organizations are extending their repertoire of ways in which they can develop staff, although the traditional classroom-based experience is still the most common, as Figure 3.4 shows. Seventy-two per cent of the responding organizations were not able to put a financial value on training.

Finally, the survey looked at benefits and obstacles. It was clear from the results that one of the key drivers is the improvement of links between training and development and strategic planning processes. Interestingly, the survey also showed that most of the benefits rated, as shown in Figure 3.5, relate to the actual training and its supporting functions. (This may well be linked to the heavy use of reaction sheets and little else.)

So why do some organizations not bother?

Experience has shown that the most common reasons for not proceeding concern the cost of the process and the potential bureaucracy. Many organizations wonder what value it adds, especially if they believe they are doing the right things already. Even organizations that are interested and see potential benefits

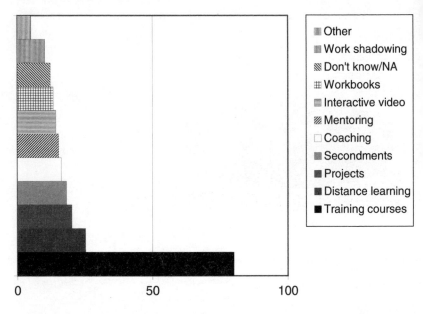

Figure 3.4 *Development areas subject to systematic evaluation*
(Source: Industrial Society, 1994*)*

frequently dither about the final decision. They often say it's the wrong time:

- 'We're too busy planning.'
- 'We have too many changes on the go at the moment.'
- 'We are in the middle of introducing ISO 9000/Business Excellence/ Total Quality.'
- 'We are in the middle of a redundancy exercise.'

Investors in People is often seen as another task rather than a tool or framework to help manage these situations. However, many of the recognized organizations successfully introduced Investors in People while dealing with the above situations. Worries about the bureaucracy stem from the perceived need for paper evidence and thick portfolios of the past, but as Chapter 6 shows, the emphasis has now completely moved away from paper being seen as 'evidence'. The focus is now on outcomes with the key question asked of the existence of process and policy being: 'So what?'

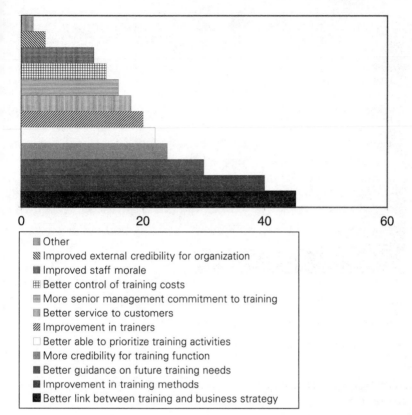

Figure 3.5 *Main benefits gained from evaluating training*
(Source: Industrial Society, 1994)

Consistent assessment

Many organizations, especially large and multi-site ones, are concerned that although Investors in People is a national standard, assessment is spread around the whole of the UK, and therefore assessors may interpret the indicators differently. While it is impossible to ensure that assessors make exactly the same judgements, many actions such as shadowing of assessors and assessor moderation meetings have been taken to ensure that as far as possible assessors are consistent. The various project reviews of Investors in People have been conscious of these concerns and have continuously tried to address them. The introduction of practitioner competences from April 2001 and the requirement for all practitioners to demonstrate that they can meet them is the latest response.

Summary

This chapter has examined some of the reasons that have influenced organizations to commit to Investors in People. It has also detailed some of the benefits quoted by organizations that have achieved recognition. It has paid particular attention to the role that Investors in People has played in increasing the evaluation of the benefits of training and development. It has looked at some of the reasons and concerns that have stopped organizations from making the commitment. The answer, therefore, to 'Why bother?' is – because it works!

The rest of the book addresses the issues associated with implementing Investors in People, to enable readers, their teams and their organizations to make up their own minds!

CHAPTER 4

The Journey

Although the Standard has been through many changes it is still essentially the same! The underpinning philosophy and ethos is the same as it always has been. That is why the journey (although the route might have changed) is still more important than the destination. In other words, as indicated throughout this book, the process as developed and implemented by the organization and its ability to deliver the required outcomes is the most significant element in the success or failure of Investors in People.

This chapter is therefore of particular importance as it explains the stages in the journey and what they involve. It answers such questions as:

- How do I start?
- How long will it take?
- How much will it cost?
- How bureaucratic is it?
- How long will it last?

There is, it will be demonstrated, clear potential for organizations to benefit from every stage of the Investors in People process. It should be remembered at all times that action being taken is to improve the organization's effectiveness, not to meet the Standard for its own sake. The Standard is based on best practice, so action to meet it should lead to improved effectiveness.

It might be helpful to offer a few words of warning for those readers seeking the ideal approach to meet the Standard. They may be disappointed to find that there is no one approach. Nevertheless, by reading the following chapters and the case study experiences in Part Three they should be able to identify appropriate methods that meet the needs of their own organization. The 'secret' is to interpret the indicators and the evidence requirements in a way that suits the culture of the organization.

How do I start?

The first thing that any organization needs to do is to find out how it currently compares with the Standard. This is where the 12 indicators and 33 evidence requirements, as reproduced in Appendix 1, come into play again, as it is against these that the comparison, often called a first or initial assessment, and sometimes called a diagnosis, should be made.

Organizations enter the process at different levels of sophistication with regard to training and development. There are also a wide variety of corporate cultures: strong, weak, directed, undirected, positive, negative, to mention but a few. For a large number of organizations the decision to make a commitment is possibly the most challenging in the whole process. It can seem like a step into the dark and may feel threatening. Indicators and evidence requirements that at first glance seem clear take on a sometimes disconcerting complexity when applied to your own organization. They may then seem confusing and give rise to concern and doubt as to how far away from meeting the Standard the organization actually is. This then leads to the question of how much time commitment actually entails.

These legitimate concerns can be offset by considering the fact that most organizations have existing systems and processes that will go some way to delivering some of the outcomes required by the indicators. Occasionally these systems and processes will be very obvious, but sometimes they need to be interpreted in order to satisfy the requirements of the indicator. Again, the focus is on the enhancement of existing good practice and the introduction of structured systemic improvements. The feedback following the first assessment should therefore take account of the potential delivery of outcomes through improvements that are already planned but perhaps not yet implemented, eg introduction of ISO 9000, the Business Excellence Model, reorganization, delayering, re-engineering and so on.

There is an often confusing array of sources of help with interpretation and guidance for organizations going through or thinking about going through the process. These included TECs up to 31st March 2001, Chambers of Commerce, Business Links, NTOs and, from 1st April 2001, the Small Business Service and local Learning and Skills Councils (LLSCs). In addition there is a wide variety of independent consultants and trainers and some colleges and universities offer a range of related programmes. (See Chapter 13 for sources of help.)

All organizations will at one time or another be raising some or all of the above questions and concerns. Investors in People provides an opportunity for them to be addressed in a coherent and consistent manner via the diagnostic stage.

How to assess where you are starting from

To answer this, the traditional method was to undertake a 'diagnostic exercise'. One of the outcomes from the STAR project (see Chapter 1) was to challenge the traditional method of diagnosis and encourage organizations to view assessment as a continuous process and therefore immediately apply for a first or initial assessment, carried out by an approved assessor. In practice this has not happened as frequently as initially anticipated. It is also clear that the method employed in carrying out the diagnostic stage varies from one area to another depending on the policy of the LLSC/TEC. However, the choice clearly rests with the organization and may be dependant on how close or how far away the organization thinks it is from meeting the Standard.

It can be tempting to give one or two people the task of examining the indicators and evidence requirements and ticking off which they think the organization meets. These people are often senior managers and include the Personnel or Training Manager. This approach may give a broad indication but it depends very heavily on the managers' knowledge and depth of understanding of the realities of the organization's corporate culture at a range of levels. Some LLSC/TEC advisers will help you do this whilst others may offer support for a consultant to help complete this 'quick and dirty' diagnosis. If it is felt that very little is in place then this approach to diagnosis may be adequate; it may be pointless to question other staff when the likely outcome will be confirmation that there is little in place to meet the requirements.

However, if it is felt that a significant number of outcomes are being delivered as required by the Standard, it is essential to involve a cross-section of staff from all levels to check this and to check that perceptions of staff are the same as the perceptions of senior managers. Experience has shown that the existence of systems and processes does not always mean they actually work and lead to the required outcomes, so be prepared for surprises.

To check out the perceptions there are two options: apply for assessment immediately (see Chapter 5); or ask for a 'traditional diagnosis' which should be carried out by a registered practitioner who may be an LLSC/TEC adviser or a consultant brought in by the LLSC/TEC. The process would normally involve selecting a representative cross-section of a diagonal slice of the organization, taking on board the various criteria set out for assessors (as described in Chapter 5).

In large or geographically diverse organizations some traditional diagnoses may also involve carrying out a confidential survey using questionnaires that have been customized to suit each individual organization. The questionnaires and/or interview questions should be designed in such a way as to determine which of the 12 indicators and 33 evidence requirements are met satisfactorily and which are not. Often at least two sets of questionnaires are used, one for managers and one for the remaining employees. These should always be adapted to suit local requirements. Using an off-the-shelf questionnaire will not help the process.

The decision about where to draw the line between who should complete the managers' survey and who should complete the employees' surveys is often not easy. Middle and junior managers could in fact complete both as they manage staff and are themselves managed. Therefore, especially in larger organizations, you could use separate surveys for middle managers/supervisors and senior managers. Examples of three types of questionnaire are in Appendices 2, 3 and 4.

Several benefits can be gained by applying for an assessment immediately including potential savings with regard to time and money. The feedback from the assessor should enable you to focus precisely on areas that need addressing, which is particularly useful if your organization is not far from meeting the Standard. If the required outcomes are demonstrated recognition will be recommended immediately. If this is not the case, the next stage depends on how great the gap is between the current situation in the areas of concern and what is required for immediate recognition. If the gap is not huge, action may be implemented quite quickly. When it is felt the gap has been addressed the assessor may be invited back and may merely revisit the areas of concern, ie the gaps, before recommending recognition. If the assessor finds significant gaps and the process to fill them takes some time the assessor may need to revisit more than just the areas for concern to check that nothing has lapsed before making a recommendation for recognition.

If your organization is quite a long way from meeting the evidence requirements there may be advantages in 'going the traditional route', especially if you are in a large organization. The authors are not convinced that there are cost savings by going for early assessment as the cost of assessment may well be more expensive than employing a consultant, particularly if the cost of a consultant is part funded by the LLSC/TEC. Organizations who are a long way from meeting the Standard frequently have many issues that require attention and the feedback from the assessor might not be in sufficient depth to address all the issues: assessors are not supposed to offer advice. External support may be needed and it is likely that any consultant brought in would need to do further research before helping to identify solutions. Clearly this would add to the cost of assessment.

Whatever approach is chosen it should involve a real cross-section of employees including critics and cynics. As well as getting a realistic analysis, involving people will start the process of gaining knowledge and understanding of what Investors in People is and how it will help the development of both individuals and the organization.

Analysing the information

Once the diagnosis is completed, particularly if there are still gaps, you will have a great deal of information about your organization. For some organizations it may be the first time this type of information has been gathered. Some of it will confirm what you already knew, some will be new to you, and some of it may contradict what you had assumed. The last category may be the most painful information to accept, especially for managers, but it is probably the most useful. If the diagnosis is carried out confidentially in a threat-free environment, your people will tell you what actually happens, not what they think you would like to hear.

In many organizations the results from the diagnosis, whether it is an assessment or a traditional diagnosis, often reveal that managers believe they are managing staff effectively. Equally often, their staff disagree, as shown in Figure 4.1.

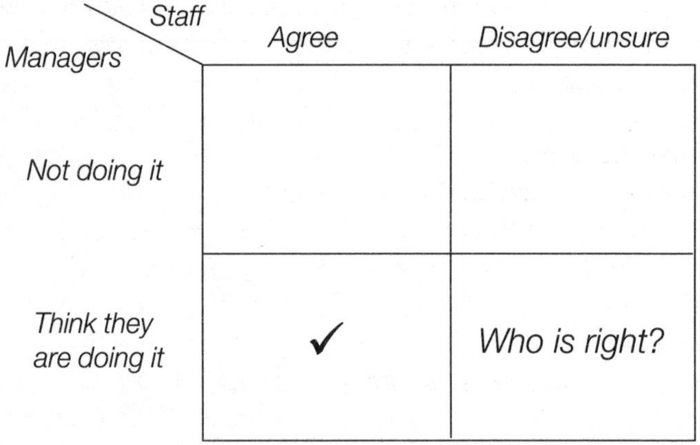

Figure 4.1 *Managers' expectations versus employees' perceptions*

The matrix in Figure 4.1 illustrates various scenarios using four boxes. In the top left both managers and employees agree that the support is not there. In the bottom left they agree that it is there. However, in the bottom right the managers think they are supporting staff while the staff don't think they are. Is it that the employee expects too much or are the managers deluding themselves? The only solution is for the managers and staff to discuss the issue. Once there is agreement, the top right box will be squeezed as the bottom left box will automatically remain a square.

Most organizations have processes and systems that appear on the surface to be working, but underneath, for a variety of reasons, are not functioning effectively and delivering the outcomes that they should. This issue, and a variety of others, will present a challenge to senior managers in particular, but having feedback presents the following opportunities: to improve the systems' effectiveness (in order to deliver the outcomes), to improve people's perceptions of the systems, and to improve working relationships.

Although the Standard, its indicators and evidence requirements are based on good practice it does not prescribe how things should be done: it merely describes the expected outcomes. This allows the Standard to be met in the way that best suits an organization. Fitness for purpose, in other words.

Of course every organization is different, but experience has shown that in general where the expected outcomes are not demonstrated one or more of the following processes will not be working effectively:

- communications;
- planning (strategic and/or short-term);
- the process for identifying development needs;
- management effectiveness;
- monitoring and evaluation.

Deciding what needs to be done

During this analytical and planning stage a number of organizations, particularly when they find they have quite a bit to do to meet the requirements of the Standard, have found it useful to set up a project team. Again the temptation may be to include only line managers in this team, but experience has shown that it is prudent to include a cross-section of people from different levels and functions; ideally they should include trade union representatives where they exist. The TUC recognizes Investors in People, and local opposition or difficulty clearly raises a number of questions over the communication process. Having a cross-sectional team will not only ensure that plans are practicable, it will also start the process of gaining commitment from the people. Experience has demonstrated that project teams can be equally effective in both large and small organizations.

Action planning

A plan should now be drawn up showing what actions are going to be taken to deliver the required outcomes. This may involve introducing new systems and processes and/or improving and maintaining existing ones. The plan should account for any improvements already arranged, ie they should be integrated into the plan and not duplicated. The plan should stipulate who is responsible for taking the action and by what stage it should be completed. Ideally it should also be cross-referenced to the indicators.

A danger encountered by many companies at this stage is to let the indicators and the evidence requirements lead the action. One action may have repercussions on a number of indicators, so it is far more effective in terms of organizational efficiency to lead by actions. Certainly both large and small organizations have benefited in this way, as illustrated in the case studies. Once the actions are completed the indicators should automatically be met. Consistency of approach is achieved by using the same assessor from commitment through recognition and beyond. The assessor will gather ever greater knowledge of the organization and increasingly assume the role of critical friend, as well as saving time and money.

Remember, when agreeing such things as process, timescale, methodology and actions that:

Investors in People works for you, not you for it.

How long does it take?

Managers in every organization at some time ask: 'How long will the whole process take?' The plan of action will answer this question. It will also indicate the level of time commitment people will be expected to make. This commitment is likely to lead to the biggest investment of resources for most organizations. However, for most organizations this extra commitment of time and resource should be reduced if the plan of action is developed in a way that integrates action to meet the Investors in People Standard with actions already planned. The average time taken has been calculated as about 18 months from commitment to recognition. This is, however, a meaningless figure. Recognition is most certainly not the end of the journey.

The other potential cost, of course, is if the internal expertise is not there or available and an external consultant is brought in. Chapter 13 looks at the sources of external help available and indeed whether such help is actually needed. (For some organizations this can be a source of concern.)

Implementing the plan

Organizations that did not initially set up a project team to help develop a plan of action are advised to set one up now. The experience of organizations in our case studies suggests that the team's role will be to:

- monitor progress towards achieving the plan;
- share the responsibility and the workload;
- share the ups and downs of the process in order to maintain progress;
- become the organization's Investors in People 'champions', ie share information, encourage and influence colleagues;
- offer advice and answer questions (members of the project team will quickly become knowledgeable about the Standard and the indicators);
- bring information from the various parts of the organization that shows where the barriers exist and where things are working effectively that will ultimately advise the group when the plan is achieved and the organization is ready for assessment.

There is a set of informal 'golden rules' for implementing the action plan. These are:

- Make sure that the leader of the project team has significant 'clout' (ie there should be clear lines of executive accountability and authority).

- Do not introduce things (especially paperwork and bureaucracy in general) that do not help your organization to improve its effectiveness.
- Ensure you get commitment from those people who have to use the new systems and processes.
- Keep things simple (ensure processes are designed in a way that meets what is needed, as they will be easier to sell in order to get commitment and to motivate people to continue).
- Challenge the traditional ways of doing things – especially when the reason for doing things this way is 'because we always have'!
- Persevere.
- Be prepared for 'slippage' (most organizations do not meet their original timetable).

Chapter 6 explains what is needed to convince an independent assessor. The requirement for paper evidence has largely gone so the need is much reduced. Remember – the only 'real' evidence comes from what people say. It's all about outcomes. Processes are much less important to the assessor than their results. It's the 'So what?' question again.

Summary

This chapter has illustrated the journey towards becoming an Investor in People. This journey entails an examination at various levels of best practice emanating from organizations that have completed the process.

   This chapter has attempted to answer a number of the most common questions, such as:

- How do we start?
- How long will it take?
- How much will it cost?
- How can the bureaucracy be kept to a minimum?

We have shown that there are potential benefits to be gained at every stage in the process and emphasized that the action being taken is to improve the organization's effectiveness and not to meet the Investors in People Standard for its own sake.

CHAPTER 5

The First Assessment Process

This chapter examines the role of assessors, what they look for and the nature and structure of the first assessment. It looks at methods of producing and presenting evidence to the assessor and what happens when the assessor visits your premises to interview staff. It examines the need for rigour during the assessment process while keeping the exercise as non-bureaucratic and cost-effective as possible. It examines the difficulties assessors sometimes face in deciding whether the Standard has been met and what happens when it is not.

The purpose of assessment

In the past, many organizations, particularly larger ones, questioned the logic of submitting themselves to external assessment. This was often because they were happy with their own training set-up or because the emphasis was – rightly – placed on the journey rather than the destination.

More recently, there has been a shift in thinking. Where an organization has spent a lot of time and effort in working towards the indicators, why not get the 'badge' to show what has been achieved? After all, external benchmarking is of increasing value in the marketplace.

It is the external benchmarking aspect that is the key here. If you don't bother to come forward for assessment how will you know whether or not you are as good as you say you are? More importantly, perhaps, how will your various stakeholders know that you are as good as you say you are?

Consider the case of Toyota: for years the company had been employing in its plants throughout the world what it believed to be sound training and developmental processes, practices and procedures. The organization had been used in case studies in numerous books and widely quoted as an example of good practice. The Toyota UK plant in Derbyshire decided it would like to come forward for assessment. One of the main reasons it gave was to test itself against the principles of the Standard. That it met the requirements both vindicates the practices of Toyota and underlines the relevance of the Standard in this context.

Managing the assessment process

Up until April 2001, the assessment process management was conducted by an Assessment Unit but from April 2001 the units who manage the assessment process became regionally based Investors in People Quality Centres. Although the structure of some of these units will vary – and the units are intended to be different from the previous Assessment Units – many of the principles described below concerning the assessment process will not. The Assessment Unit selects, develops and manages the assessors. This involves:

- sponsoring assessors (ie being responsible for their training and development, satisfying the practitioner Performance Review Framework criteria and ensuring that they carry out the required number of assessments to maintain their 'licence to assess', and that they take part in meetings to share problems and discuss good practice);
- developing internal processes that assure the quality of assessments as they take place;
- internally verifying all assessments (this will involve ensuring that the assessor carries out the job effectively, and checking the quality of the report to the panel).

So every assessor has to be registered with a unit. When an organization is ready for assessment it should let its local LLSC/TEC adviser know, who then makes the necessary arrangements with the Assessment Unit. The Assessment Unit will then appoint an assessor. There is also a National Assessment Unit based at Investors in People UK. This unit was set up initially to manage the assessments of large and multi-site organizations, and also assessed the TECs. There are a number of national assessors based within the unit.

The assessor's role

The role of the assessor is to check that there is evidence that the organization meets the requirements of the Investors in People Standard and all the constituent indicators and evidence requirements. Traditionally this was done by ensuring that systems and processes were in place, that they worked in practice and that the staff of the organization were aware of them and agreed that they worked.

The revisions to the Standard have increased the emphasis on the need for evidence that systems and processes work and deliver outcomes. Illustrations of training and development or learning that has taken place are required. These will include verbal evidence demonstrating that people believe that Investors in People is working effectively, ie that there is a commitment, that needs are identified, actioned and evaluated, etc.

The assessors' role is to help the organization to prove it meets the requirements. Assessors should allow organizations every opportunity to seek and present additional evidence, where it exists, at any time throughout the process. The emphasis is seen as being on encouragement rather than restriction. This is an extremely important aspect of the Standard and one that often gets overlooked by organizations as they prepare for assessment. The assessor is looking for evidence that demonstrates that the principles of Investors in People are in operation. If he or she does not find it with the first batch of interviewees, more will be interviewed until either evidence is found or it is clear the organization must do more work in that area of concern.

Who are the assessors?

Assessors are generally drawn from two groups: staff from LLSC TECs/LECs (or in Northern Ireland, the T&EA) and staff from training and development consultancies or units. To become an assessor it is necessary to have a background in training and development and an understanding of how business works. Assessors have to follow an introductory training course and then undertake a range of developmental activities to be granted and thereafter to retain their 'licence'. These activities include shadowing an experienced assessor on an assessment, working with experienced advisers, and being shadowed by an experienced assessor when conducting their first assessment. From April 2001 instead of using existing NVQ standards E11 and E31, they have to demonstrate that they meet the requirements of a set of criteria laid out in the Performance Review Framework that Investors in People UK have developed and piloted.

Once accredited, to maintain their 'licence' to assess, assessors must carry out a minimum of three assessments per year and undergo a development review with the assessment unit's Development Manager. As part of their continual professional development they are also expected to attend assessor meetings for development activities, to share experiences and discuss difficult cases.

What the assessor expects

When an organization comes forward for assessment the assessor expects that information will be presented either in writing or verbally in a way that enables him or her to understand:

- the organization;
- its function;
- its structure;
- information about employees to assist with the selection of the interviewees;
- how the organization believes it meets each of the indicators that form the national standard.

It is helpful for the assessor to see any planning documentation in advance but this is not absolutely essential (see overleaf).

Some organizations still find it helpful to prepare a storyboard. Those who do should concentrate on describing how the evidence requirements that concern the organization, top management and managers are met. It is probably pointless addressing evidence requirements that start with the word people, as the only way to validate what is claimed is for the assessor to speak to the people.

Presenting your case

Until recently the normal process was to present your case using evidence gathered together in a ring-binder, which is referred to as a portfolio of evidence. Readers already familiar with the NVQ process will have experienced portfolios of evidence.

A portfolio has never been a requirement but has always been considered the most appropriate method, as it can help in setting the scene for the assessor. There has been some criticism in some areas of excessive focusing on portfolio production; indeed many assessors believe that 'going in cold' to the site visit interviews might well be better in some cases, especially where there is no business need for the organization to produce such information in the form of a portfolio. The STAR project (see Chapter 1) served to remind everyone that the assessment process does not require a portfolio, and since the completion of that project most organizations have chosen not to produce portfolios.

Why do some organizations still prepare a portfolio?

A few organizations feel that the portfolio is still the most appropriate way of presenting their case. Quite often these are larger and/or more complex organizations that have a great deal of 'naturally occurring' paperwork which they believe can demonstrate their case.

Some smaller organizations have found the discipline of producing a portfolio has been helpful. It reinforces how much they have achieved in a physical way and occasionally can also be used to impress an internal audience. For some organizations the production of a portfolio is useful as it is the first time they have collated policies and guidelines, procedures and systems, etc.

The message is clear: if you feel a portfolio will be useful you have the option of continuing to present your case in this way, however it may result in extra work for the assessor and this may mean extra costs to the organization.

Alternative approaches

As emphasis has moved away from portfolios the following approaches have been tried:

- using marketing and promotional material as background reading;
- looking at Web sites;
- compiling storyboards with minimal written material, eg written plans, individual development plans and/or reviews or appraisals;
- having individuals or top management teams give verbal presentations;
- using videos, such as staff communications videos;
- sitting in on induction events.

From the assessment process to initial recognition

The STAR project, offering early and staged assessment (see Chapter 1), has provided assessors with greater flexibility. The majority of first assessments comprise the following stages although the process may vary slightly from one area to another.

The Investors in People Quality Centre now has the responsibility for the appointment of assessors. In Scotland, Investors in People Scotland acts as the Investors in People Quality Centre for the whole country. The assessor will make contact with an organization to arrange to make preliminary agreement about the assessment process. This process will depend on whether the organization has decided to produce a portfolio of evidence or not.

Without a portfolio

Where the organization has opted not to produce a portfolio the assessor will need to be very flexible. He or she will initially enquire, probably by telephone, how the organization intends presenting its case and will make the necessary arrangements for assessment. This may still involve a preliminary visit, or basic information being sent by post to allow the assessor to choose an interview sample. For very small organizations, however, the arrangements may simply be to agree a date for the on-site visit to take place and the assessor will make a choice for interview from the available people and gather the evidence throughout the visit.

In larger organizations the next stage is normally the selection of people for interview. This selection will be based on the factors shown in Figure 5.1. People should be chosen to give a representative cross-section, including a diagonal representation, ie not interviewing all from one line manager, and consideration must be given to gender, age, ethnicity and disability. A question often asked is: 'How many people will be interviewed?' It is difficult to answer as the precise number of employees and percentage interviewed

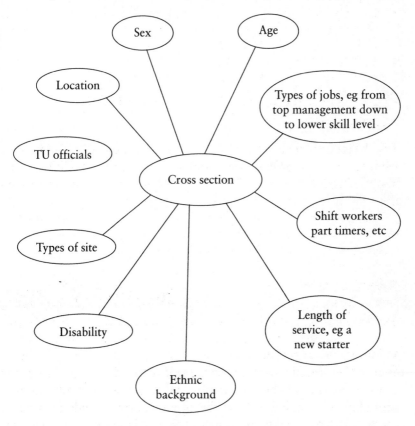

Figure 5.1 *The interviews: who do you include?*

will vary from one organization to another depending on the complexity and diversity of the organization, its products and related functions and the assessor's own professional judgement. A general rule, however, is the smaller the organization, the higher the percentage of people selected. Investors in People UK have produced a guide for assessors and assessment units. This is reproduced as Appendix 5.

The assessor will ask for a room to be allocated to carry out the interviews. The interviews must be conducted sensitively and confidentially. They will be a mixture of one-to-one interviews and group interviews. Group interviews will normally be for teams or for staff across the organization who perform similar roles. Assessors will use a variety of methods such as informal 'walk-abouts', observing team briefings, management meetings, training sessions, etc. However, it is generally still the one-to-one interviews that provide the best information. Telephone interviews can also be used where appropriate, such as in an organization with a very large number of sites with small numbers of staff spread over a wide geographical area.

The assessor will decide who to interview but will generally leave it to the organization to arrange matters in such a way as to avoid unnecessary disruption to the normal working practices. The exception to this is the usual request to meet with the head of the organization first thing on day one of the site visit. If shift working is in operation it is likely that the assessor will want to interview during the selected shifts. If the organization employs people on different locations the assessor will also need to visit some or all of these locations.

With a portfolio

On the rare occasions when an organization presents a portfolio of evidence, the assessor will normally arrange a visit to pick up the portfolio and check dates for the site visit(s). The assessor may also ask for a short tour of the site and/or ask to be talked through the portfolio by the person who compiled it.

The assessor will then take the portfolio away and carry out a 'desk-top review' which will examine the evidence presented and compare it against each indicator and the evidence requirements. After the desk-top review the assessor will be able to decide what the issues for discussion on site will be and who needs be interviewed. The process will then follow that outlined above.

The site visits

The purpose of site visits is for the assessor to check with the employees at all levels that what the organization thinks is happening is happening. This may be what has been described verbally or in the storyboard.

Details of what the assessor is looking for is outlined in Chapters 8, 9 and 10. Briefly the assessor will ask questions to establish that:

- people believe that the organization is committed to developing its people and that the commitment extends to all people;
- people understand what the organization is trying to achieve and can see how their job contributes to its success;
- people can provide illustrations that confirm their development needs are reviewed on a regular basis;
- development action that has been identified as needed actually takes place;
- discussion takes place to ensure that employees know exactly what they are supposed to learn to do, and that after the event they review how they are actually applying the new skill or knowledge, or take further action as appropriate;
- people feel valued and feel that their contribution is recognized by the organization.

After the site visit

The final stages of the process are similar whether or not a portfolio has been produced. After completing the site visits the assessor will analyse the evidence, comparing it with the indicators and the evidence requirements and, if satisfied that all are met, prepare a report recommending to the Recognition Panel that recognition as an Investor in People is awarded.

The next chapter describes the recognition process. Later in this chapter we describe what happens when the assessor is not convinced that the organization meets the Standard.

Difficulties faced by assessors

The assessor needs to be able to understand how different organizations may have interpreted the indicators and the evidence requirements differently. The standard allows this flexibility in order to meet differing business requirements or organizational cultures. Unless care has been taken in presenting the case, an assessor may have difficulty with particular interpretations. For example, methods used to interpret how development needs are identified in an educational establishment will be quite different to the methods used in manufacturing. Business planning methodologies differ from one organization to another; some do not refer to 'business planning' but to 'operational' planning or 'strategic development' planning, for example. Although assessors are expected to be able to handle these situations, a careful presentation of the evidence, clarifying meaning, can speed up the process.

It is interesting to note that where there is on-the-job development, people do not always recognize it as training or development and frequently have difficulty explaining how they acquired new skills or knowledge. Quite often they say they 'picked it up' but often cannot or do not clarify how. The assessor will try a number of approaches to identify where this occurs, but organizations that use this approach to development should give assessors sufficient information to enable them to check that it does actually happen. Assessors often suggest at feedback that the organization might wish to make employees more aware of what development actually comprises for their organization.

Probably the most difficult decision that an assessor will face concerns those organizations that are borderline cases. The assessor needs to decide whether they are doing enough to meet the requirements of the Standard. The focus on outcomes should make it easier but in practice does not. The situations that cause most difficulty are when processes are informal and/or continual and not recorded in any way. Assessors have always had a degree of discomfort particularly when the process for identifying development needs was informal and unwritten. At times they have felt uncertain and unconvinced that the systems are working or perhaps that they even exist. This situation is not helped when organizations have rightly been told that 'you don't need formal systems, just the ability of people to describe outcomes'. However, when relying purely on memory, the description of the outcome may be vague. It may be even more difficult if some 'pre-assessment' activity has been carried out and it was felt that the organization met the Standard and therefore clearly felt that these informal systems were working. Remember it is the outcome that the assessor is looking for but the outcome will need a process or system to deliver it. So why is it difficult and why do assessors often feel unconvinced?

There are many cases when informal systems *are* working very effectively and outcomes *are* being delivered and this is usually quite clear from the interviews. People can actually describe how their line manager developed them – perhaps without even realizing it they describe a structured but unbureaucratic process that their manager followed. If pushed they can also illustrate with an example (or examples) the structure that identified each development need, agreed what action would take place and the follow-up after the action to see that it had been effective. With a little coaxing some managers can also describe the process and its outcomes, again perhaps not realizing that the process was structured.

However, there are other occasions when people use vague phrases – 'it happens all the time' or 'it happens continuously' but often struggle to illustrate the statement with examples. Managers often say their 'door was always open' and staff say the manager was 'always there if needed' but again are unable to convince the assessor with examples that confirmed that managers actually supported and encouraged staff development.

The doubts can also be increased, especially in small or growing organizations where much of the management or supervisory development had been in-house and on-the-job. Frequently in these type of organizations many people have never experienced the benefits of structured processes and perhaps have little expectation. Here people are often positive about 'support' from their line manager when in reality there may be little support in the terms that assessors are seeking. To an experienced assessor it often feels that there is an air of 'subconscious incompetence' about manager's actions and staff expectations. When managers and/or staff have experience of larger organizations and probably have been developed by those organizations they have a better feel for what support they should give or expect.

On the other hand the doubts could be increased if some of those interviewed had come from larger organizations, were used to formal processes and perhaps unreasonably expected a more formal process. Occasionally they are seen by some managers as being awkward or having unrealistic expectations.

All in all it can leave assessors in a situation where they have to make a decision with little factual information and if they are not convinced it can make it more difficult to feed back why they're not convinced. In some cases this feedback may be needed to convince both the organization and the LLSC/TEC adviser, who may quite rightly say a number of times that the Standard does not require formality. Assessors in this situation may well be left with conflicting thoughts about the decision. They may feel they're right but may ask: 'Are these people still seeking bureaucracy?' or 'Are they expecting too much?'

The answer may be that there is a lack of 'structure' to the process. Informal does not mean unstructured. This leads to more questions for assessors to consider. Is it right to look for structure? Is it good enough to accept people's word that it happens all the time? Is it right to seek further examples? If assessors do this will they be seen to be too rigorous? Feedback to one assessor who assessed a school was 'that staff felt it wasn't as bad as an OFSTED inspection, but not far off!'

The Standard has always been about effectiveness – perhaps another word for outcomes – and many experienced assessors have developed themselves away from process-based questions to outcomes-based questions. However, the old Standard was still fairly process-based and therefore often evidence was process-based.

The question to consider is: 'With an outcomes-based Standard will organizations and their advisers be able to present their case for recognition without structure?' Organizations need to be warned that with informality there is a price – a more rigorous interview.

Another frequent cause of doubt for assessors is a lack of consistency. With or without formality consistency can be viewed as subjective by organizations who think they meet the Standard.

Assessors, and Recognition Panels, do not, of course, expect perfection in organizations and their systems. However, some organizations may recognize that the outcomes from processes and systems could be improved upon. This should not prevent them from applying for assessment. As long as at the time of the assessment there is sufficient to satisfy the assessor that each of the indicators and evidence requirements is satisfied. (See Chapters 8, 9 and 10.)

What happens when the assessor is not convinced?

If the assessor, after giving the organization every chance to provide sufficient evidence of outcomes, is still not convinced that the indicators and evidence requirements have been satisfied, he or she will recommend that the organization has not yet met all the requirements of the Standard. In practice this allows the organization more time to take further action to satisfy the indicators and provide evidence requirements. How long this will take will differ from one assessment to another depending on the pertinent issues. Some issues may only take a couple of weeks to rectify but in the main the process will take a few months. When this happens the assessor will provide a report showing which indicators are not satisfied and present the report to the organization with a representative of the TEC/LLSC/LEC in attendance. The TEC/LLSC/LEC should then be able to offer and arrange support for the organization to take the required action.

With the advent of the concept of the staged or continuous assessment process many organizations come forward for an early or first assessment as an initial diagnosis or to check how they are progressing. For these organizations the fact that they are not yet meeting the requirements of the Standard is not a shock. Sometimes the shock may be that in spite of doubts they do actually meet the Standard and recognition as an Investor in People will be recommended. The difficulty arises for assessors when organizations think they meet the Standard but the assessor finds that they do not.

Assessments which do not lead to a positive recommendation for recognition do not normally go to the Recognition Panel. It is critical to the underpinning values of the Investors in People process that organizations are not made to feel that not yet meeting the Standard is a failure. A lot of work will probably have been put into the process and quite clearly the organization will be disappointed.

Most organizations in this situation have usually met most of the requirements and are therefore not failures. Some household names have found themselves in this position and would clearly not wish to be considered failures.

Summary

This chapter has examined the process and purpose of the first assessment. It has described the options organizations have in presenting their case to the assessor. It has reflected good practice but also highlighted the areas of difficulty assessors may be faced with. It has described what happens when organizations do not demonstrate that they have met the requirements of the Standard and its indicators. Finally, the concept of a staged or continuous assessment has been outlined.

CHAPTER 6

The Recognition Process

This chapter examines the history and role of the panel and its function within the quality assurance process of Investors in People. It also runs through the structure of the recognition panel and the related recognition processes and activities. It describes who the recognition panel members are. It also looks at the changes that have taken place in the assessment, recognition and quality assurance processes

This chapter will be of particular value to those approaching recognition or re-recognition, those seeking an overview of the process, and to trainers and students.

Why have a Recognition Panel?

The previous chapter explained the assessment process and concluded with the assessor preparing a report to the Recognition Panel. Why can the assessor not make the decision? Why have a Recognition Panel? There have always been two clear answers as follows.

Firstly, it is an integral part of the quality assurance process to check that the assessor has done a good professional job and can convince the panel that the organization does meet the Standard. Secondly, it has always been the intention that the decision to recognize organizations should be made by their peers.

The role of the Recognition Panel is to ensure that:

- all stages of the assessment have been properly carried out;
- satisfactory evidence has been provided to the assessor in support of all elements of the standard;
- the organization is sufficiently free-standing as a business unit to be properly assessed;
- recognitions are consistent over time.

In other words, the panel exists to maintain the consistency and protect the integrity of both the Standard and the LLSC/TEC.

The STAR project (see Chapter 1) raised the issue of allowing assessors to decide whether organizations should achieve recognition. The outcome was that the panel would retain its role of deciding whether to accept the assessors' recommendations. However, there was an acceptance that experienced assessors were competent and that panels will continue to make the decision for *first assessments only*, with assessors making the decision as to whether organizations should retain their recognition. The role of the Recognition Panel will therefore be broadened, as outlined later in this chapter.

Who sits on the Recognition Panel?

The arrangement (to April 2001) for Recognition Units was virtually identical to those for Assessment Units (see Chapter 5) with some based in a single TEC and others set up by and serving the needs of a number of TECs. As with Assessment Units, from April 2001 their role is subsumed within the regionally based Investors in People Quality Centres.

The Centre is responsible for:

- the recruitment of panel members;
- managing Recognition Panels (ie training and developing members);
- drawing up quality procedures that ensure that panel members have the reports on time, that panels are quorate, etc.

Historically, the precise membership of Recognition Panels varied from Recognition Unit to Recognition Unit but had to include at least two senior people. They would typically be local employers, including some TEC Board members and senior personnel and training professionals. As the number of recognitions has increased, most Recognition Units have started to include on the panel people who work for companies that had gone through the process and were recognized as Investors in People. This has now been formalized with the rule that 'all panels must be comprised of two senior people from recognized organizations'. Panel members were, and will continue to be, unpaid and should be independent and impartial.

There are procedures in place to be triggered where there is a potential conflict of interest, such as a Recognition Panel member's company coming up for recognition, or an employer who has a contractual relationship with a specific LLSC. In the past these cases the assessment and recognition process were handled by another Recognition Unit. With the advent of the nine regional Quality Centres in England and Wales the existing rules continue but there should be less variation.

Arrangements in Scotland

In Scotland assessment and recognition arrangements have differed from those in England and Wales for some time.

Investors in People Scotland is a company limited by guarantee established to carry out assessments and arrange the recognition of Scottish organizations on behalf of Local Enterprise Companies (LECs), the Scottish equivalents of TECs. The Scottish Recognition Panels are held alternately in the Highlands and the Lowlands and are constituted in a similar manner to the above Recognition Panels.

Arrangements in Northern Ireland

There are no LLSCs/TECs (or LECs) in Northern Ireland, where Investors in People is administered by the Training and Employment Agency (T&EA). The assessment and recognition process is very similar to that in England and Wales however, with the Agency taking responsibility. There is a Northern Ireland Recognition Panel, which is constituted in a similar way to those in Britain, with the decision to recognize being made by representatives of Northern Irish employing organizations.

The National Recognition Panel

A National Recognition Panel has been in existence since the inception of Investors in People. The original role of this panel was to recognize those national multi-site organizations that chose to be assessed by national assessors employed by Investors in People UK. In practice, apart from a number of Government departments, few organizations have chosen this route, historically preferring to have worked with their local TEC. The national assessors and the National Recognition Panel have, therefore, concentrated in the main on assessing and recognizing TECs, some LECs and NTOs. The National Recognition Panel is constituted in a similar way to the regional ones, with its membership being drawn from the Board of Investors in People UK.

How does a Recognition Panel work?

Assessment reports are circulated to panel members early enough to allow them time for reading and preparation.

In the past the assessor was invited to present his or her report, highlighting key information. The assessor in a sense became an advocate for the organization, arguing the case for recognition. This was especially significant in borderline cases. The panel members questioned the assessor about the assessment process. It also sought justification that the organization met all the requirements of the Standard. It is important to note that panels were not allowed to revisit the evidence, so they were reliant on the assessor describing in general terms how certain requirements were met.

Following the questioning, the assessor would normally be asked to leave while panel members discussed the presentation and reached a decision. The chair of the panel recorded the decision of the panel confirming that the TEC would liaise with the assessor on a date for feedback to the organization.

As the volume of assessments rose panels were put under strain. Pilots were carried out to reduce the need for experienced assessors always to present their recommendation in person to the panel. In these cases the panel members would examine the assessor's report and make the decision on that basis. They retained the right to ask to see the assessor and in any case would expect to see the assessor make a presentation periodically.

Since the completion of the STAR project a number of variations on the above processes have been introduced. In some Recognition Units experienced assessors did not always present the report in person although a number operated in the traditional way. In those that do not the panel members still saw all reports recommending recognition and the panel that made the final decision. If panel members had questions they usually contacted the assessor by telephone. Many panels continued to have reports of the first assessments of new assessors presented to them. From April 1, 2001, the variations are likely to be fewer although, as many Assessment and Recognition Units are merging to form Regional Quality Centres, some compromises on procedures may take place but the variations again should be few.

The Recognition Panel's role and the recognition process

The panel's role has traditionally been divided into five distinct but complementary areas:

- recognizing organizations;
- quality assurance;
- dissemination of good practice;
- maintaining momentum;
- individual feedback.

The role of and future of Recognition Panels has often been discussed. Although many of the traditional roles have not changed, Investors in People UK now describe their role as:

- adding and creating value – through giving additional feedback whenever possible;
- giving credibility – through the involvement of senior people from recognized organizations;
- ensuring quality of delivery – ensuring consistency, quality assuring and developing practitioners;
- contributing to policy.

As already mentioned, it is the panel and the panel alone that has the authority to recognize an organization as an Investor in People, although this is not the case for re-recognitions. The responsibilities of the assessor conclude with the examination of the evidence and the recommendation to the panel. There are no appeal procedures of any kind and the decision of the panel is final.

As indicated above, in support of the aim of ensuring consistency, members of Recognition Panels must undertake specific training. In addition, where Recognition Panels physically meet they are also attended by a moderator, whose role includes among other things ensuring that the panel remains within its parameters.

The Recognition Panel's role post-recognition

Recognized organizations must come forward for a post-recognition review (formerly known as a re-assessment and still referred to as a re-assessment in various parts of the UK) at least once every three years. They can choose to come forward more regularly and in practice a number of organizations find it useful to be reviewed more or less annually.

When an assessor carrying out a post-recognition review finds that the organization is not continuing to meet the Standard there is a procedure to help it retain recognition. This procedure is detailed in the companion volume to this book, *Investors in People Maintained* (2001).

Ultimately if organizations do not meet the requirements of the Standard after an agreed time recognition will be taken away. Only the Panel can do this. Removal of recognition is a final option; the ethos of Investors in People is to assist the organization as much as possible to retain recognition without compromising the credibility and integrity of the Standard.

The future

The role of the Recognition Panel has been, and will continue to be, a constant source of debate. Although it is clear that the continued involvement of employers in some capacity is essential, there are some who think that the panel system may not be the best way of doing this.

Summary

This chapter has examined the role and mechanics of the Recognition Panel and how the role has developed over the years. It has described the various types of Recognition Panels and their members and the role of the Regional Quality Centre in the Recognition process.

CHAPTER 7

Investors in People in Large and Multi-site Organizations

This chapter examines some of the issues facing large and multi-site organizations and offers some thoughts on how to proceed in working towards Investors in People status. The decision for large multi-site organizations to work towards Investors in People status has proved much more complex than was originally anticipated. Although many organizations of this type adopt good practice, their size and scope makes the process difficult to administer. Many organizations believe they have adopted elements of good practice but fail to see what is in it for them. Others, such as BT and National Westminster Bank, made a commitment to work towards meeting the requirements of the national Standard and have either been recognized as a whole or in parts.

A series of government ministers stated that government departments and their agencies must commit and work towards Investors in People status by 2000 and a considerable number of these units have been recognized: the Labour Party itself, many government departments, OFSTED, the Higher Education Funding Council for England, many local authorities, NHS Trusts.

The background

Since Investors in People was first launched there have been a number of attempts to develop workable and meaningful guidelines that would encourage large and multi-site organizations to commit to the initiative. These guidelines needed to ensure the process was rigorous but fair; weighing costs against benefits. During late 1997 the guidelines were reviewed and, following consultation, revised. The guidelines, summarized below, were agreed by the Board of Investors in People UK in May 1998.

Organization recognition strategies

The Investors in People UK Board confirmed findings that:

> The Investors in People Standard is about the top management of whole organisations integrating their business strategy, business planning, and development of people to achieve improvements in their business performance. Only by working with this approach will organisations secure for themselves, and for the national economy, the maximum possible competitive advantage. The Standard is not about fragmented parts of larger organisations with limited delegated authority and autonomy achieving recognition as a mark of their own separate conformity to the Standard. Such an approach is likely to have limited organisational benefits; be expensive in terms of assessment; and cause public confusion regarding the use of the Investors in People 'badge'. It is for these reasons that organisations of whatever size or complexity should be encouraged to work towards recognition as Investors in People as whole organisations.

The options

For those large and multi-site organizations that wish to proceed the current guidelines set out two options: working towards the Standard as a whole organization; taking a 'building block' approach.

What is the 'whole organization'?

In most cases, the whole organization will be clear (eg a county council, a government department, a chain of building society branches, a chain of supermarkets, a university, the Church of England). However, in some cases with complex holding company arrangements, it will be necessary to try and build as full a picture as possible of the ownership of the organization wishing to work with the Standard. Advisers are expected to check with the next level up in the ownership chain to find out whether a strategy is in place or being considered. If the parent organization does not wish, at this stage, to work with the Standard, and gives the subsidiary organization its authority to do so, then the lower level organization can come forward for assessment and seek recognition. This organization can then be defined as the 'whole organization' for the purposes of this guidance.

Overarching recognition strategies

Organizations wishing to work towards recognition using the building block approach are encouraged to agree an overarching recognition strategy with the lead LLSC/LEC/T&EA/Investors in People UK (normally a lead LLSC is the LLSC nearest an organization's head office). The purpose behind an overarching recognition strategy is to help ensure that:

- eventually all parts of the organization will be covered by the Investors in People Standard;
- the organization works with the Standard in a cost-effective way;
- other LLSCs/LECs understand how the organization intends to work with the Standard and are able to work in partnership with the whole organization.

The overarching recognition strategy should be a 'living' document signed-off by an appropriate senior person at the top of the whole organization, usually the chief executive (or equivalent). It should be reviewed regularly (at least once each year) and revised as the organization changes and as the organization's experience of working with the Standard grows. The strategy should set out:

- which building blocks within the whole organization will be coming forward for assessment, and over what period of time;

- an agreement on how the organization intends to use the Investors in People logo for building blocks that achieve recognition. The use of the logo should not imply recognition for those parts of the organization not recognized. The Investors in People plaque will make clear the precise identity of the recognized organizational unit and similar care will be expected in the use of the logo on stationery, adverts, etc;
- how frequently post-recognition reviews will be carried out for recognized building blocks in order to maintain momentum prior to recognition of the whole organization.

The building block approach

This approach was developed in response to the growing view that the responsibility for progression should rest with the organization. One of the authors was closely involved with the development of a model that anticipated the building block approach – the Internal Quality Award. This model was used by higher education establishments and the Church of England, among others. Readers interested in reviewing this model can access a description of the approach and look at the evidence matrix produced by Loughborough University's Pilkington Library on the Internet by visiting http://www.lboro.ac.uk/service/sd/iipinhe/iipinhe.htm

Some large organizations may wish to move towards recognition on a subsidiary, departmental or divisional basis. This building block approach is an acceptable way of working towards whole organization recognition and, wherever possible, should be managed within an overall recognition strategy.

When deciding which sub-unit can be termed a 'block', the organization will need to ensure that each sub-unit is able to: have its own plan with clear aims and objectives; develop its people in line with these aims and objectives.

Whole organization recognition

A whole organization cannot be recognized as an Investor in People until it been assessed as a whole. Recognition of the whole organization depends on, in addition to recognition of all of the building blocks, a strategic assessment by the lead assessor to confirm the senior management's commitment to Investors in People and its principles across the whole organization. The rationale for this strategic assessment is that the maximum benefits of Investors in People can only be gained if it is seen and used as a strategic tool by the senior management. This strategic assessment, which can be carried out over a period of time, therefore comprises:

- a review of the organization's strategic plan and mission/vision or broad aims;
- a discussion with the chief executive (or equivalent) to confirm the overall commitment to the principles of Investors in People within the whole organization;
- a follow-on discussion about how the principles of Investors in People are applied across the whole organization. This discussion will involve appropriate members of the top management team at the centre of the organization responsible for strategic planning, people issues and systems in the whole organization.

The lead assessor will be expected to identify audit trails from the strategic assessment that can be followed through in building block assessments and vice versa.

The discussions with the senior managers at the centre of the organization are in relation to their responsibilities for the whole organization, not as in their role as heads of 'building blocks' for which they may be interviewed separately.

Whole organization recognition routes

There are two routes for organizations using the building block approach to be recognized as a whole. The first is via first assessment, when those parts of the whole organization not yet recognized come forward for assessment as one building block. This should be combined, if it has not already been, with the strategic assessment of the senior management team. The lead assessor will consider the currency of evidence collected earlier in recognized units and seek additional evidence where appropriate.

The second route is at the time of post-recognition review, when all the building blocks are recognized, the whole organization comes forward for review rather than individual building blocks. The review should include a strategic assessment of the top management team.

Investors in People UK have set two rules as follows: a whole organization cannot be recognized as a whole until it has been assessed as a single entity; recognition of the whole organization replaces all previous building block recognitions and can only be awarded by a Recognition Panel.

Resource issues

It is also important for organizations of this type to consider the resource implications of working towards the Standard separately from being assessed against the Standard.

Although it is more costly, organizations using a building block approach to work towards the Standard on a site by site or business unit by business unit basis have in the past been able to attract more financial support from TECs, than if they went forward as a whole. However, this funding is unlikely to be directly available under the LLSC regime. One of the advantages of going forward in smaller 'chunks' is that the more advanced parts of the organization, provided they are autonomous within the guidelines, are not going to be held up by the less advanced; they can then become exemplars within the organization. A danger is that if care is not taken in developing the organizational strategy, some parts of the organization may be left out on a limb because they do not satisfy the autonomy rules and therefore cannot stand alone.

It is also quite possible to choose to work towards the standard in 'bite-sized chunks' and then be assessed as a whole. There may also be advantages in doing the opposite, provided it meets the business requirements of the organization.

The implications for the assessment process being carried out on a site by site or business unit by business unit basis are that this approach will be much more expensive than having a whole organization assessment. Going forward for assessment as a whole organization would involve just one portfolio (if that method of presenting the case was chosen – see Chapter 6) and a representative selection of sites visited. On a building block approach to assessment people in each 'block' would need to present their case and many more sites would be visited.

Therefore another advantage of the building block approach is that every 'block' is assessed individually, ensuring that the Investors in People processes are delivering outcomes throughout the whole organization. The benefits of Investors in People being effective throughout the organization should outweigh the increased cost of assessment.

Whatever approach is agreed it is important that the organization feels able to meet the Standard in a way that suits its needs. However, when it comes to assessment the Standard must still be met.

Other considerations

When choosing the approach to both implementation and assessment other considerations concern:

- the degree of centralization of policies and freedom to operate within them in the organization;
- whether each site is different or are merely clones of one another;
- the issue of split head office sites.

The issues for large and multi-site organizations

Although the issues are the same for both large and small organizations, scale presents a problem for large organizations. For example, in a 10-person organization communications should not be too difficult, but in an organization that is large and/or geographically spread out it becomes an issue.

In tackling communications, a number of large organizations have gone down the route of monthly videos, newsletters on e-mail to supplement team briefings, or similar communication cascade methods. Instantaneous feedback can be had from staff in small organizations, but is much more difficult to achieve and can often be filtered in large organizations.

Communicating commitment from the top is difficult and is frequently reliant on line management in large organizations, although many senior managers do try to operate a variant on 'managing by walking about'.

On the other hand many large organizations do have, perhaps have had for some time, many policies backed up by quite structured systems, often greater resources and facilities, etc. On the downside, the collation of information, from evaluation for example, can be more difficult.

Examples of approaches by large organizations

A number of large organizations have already made policy decisions on how they should proceed with Investors in People and many have been recognized and some re-recognized.

Unilever

From the very early stages of Investors in People, Unilever took an interest in its development through Trevor Thomas, then Director of Personnel, and a member of the NTTF sub-group. Consequently they took an early decision to encourage all individual sites within their business units, such as Birds Eye Walls and Brooke Bond Foods, to work with their local TEC and progress towards Investors in People status. Two of their companies – Elida Gibbs (now Elida Fabergé) and Unilever Colworth Laboratories – were among the first 28 to be recognized. Since then most of their sites have achieved Investors in People status and been re-recognized, with the remainder working towards it.

Interestingly, early in the implementation stages, although the organization decided to go site by site, representatives from individual units networked regularly to support one another and share best practice.

WH Smith Group; Boots the Chemist

These are examples of large organizations that decided to progress with Investors in People on a business unit by business unit basis.

However, at the time of recognition both WH Smith Retail (ie the high street shops employing 13,000 people) and Boots the Chemist (employing 54,000 people) had a strong corporate identity and centrally controlled human resource policy. Each shop was a 'clone' of the other; the only variation being the size of the branches. They have both since been re-recognized.

National Westminster Bank

The National Westminster Bank took a more cautious approach. National Westminster Bank Home Loans Division, based in Bristol, is a self-contained unit. It made a commitment to Avon TEC at a fairly early stage and the rest of the organization sat back and watched with interest. In effect this unit's involvement was a pilot within the organization and the fact that the whole of National Westminster Bank made a commitment to work towards Investors in People status indicates that the pilot was very successful. Subsequently other parts of NatWest, eg Retail Banking, have been recognized. The purchase of NatWest by the Royal Bank of Scotland has led to a review of the implications of the purchase as both organizations are recognized.

British Telecom

In spite of being the largest organization to achieve Investors in People status, BT, which employed 120,000 people, opted for the whole organization approach to both implementation and assessment.

Government departments

During his term of office Michael Heseltine committed all government departments and their agencies to become Investors in People by 2000. Although this target has by no means been achieved, considerable progress has been made. Like other large or multi-site organizations, the departments and agencies had to decide the approach according to their size and complexity. For example the Ministry of Defence, after long deliberation, chose the building block approach, as did the Department for Education and Employment. The Employment Service chose the whole organization approach.

For those who moved to agency status, Investors in People offered a ready framework within which they could manage the changes. Many have now been recognized.

Other public sector organizations

Many other public sector organizations have made the commitment to work towards the Investors in People Standard. These include local authorities, NHS Trusts, schools, universities, colleges and police forces.

All have had to work through the options for implementation and assessment. Some have used a building block approach, others have taken a whole organization approach. Many have been recognized either in part or as a whole. Some are included in the case studies later in this book.

Summary

This chapter has reviewed the options and guidelines for large and multi-site organizations. It has described what whole organization assessment and recognition means. It has included illustrations of large organizations, both public and private, that have committed to Investors in People, many of which have been recognized.

CHAPTER 8

The Organization

This chapter and the following two chapters are essential reading. In them we examine the indicators and the evidence requirements, grouping them under several headings to simplify matters. The following questions will be addressed:

- What is the purpose of the indicators and evidence requirements, and the rationale for having them?;
- How do they link with one another?;
- Do they overlap?;
- What will an assessor look for?;
- Is there an audit trail through the indicators?

The complete list of the indicators and the evidence requirements is included as Appendix 1.

This chapter concentrates on the requirements of the organization especially in connection with planning and evaluation. It examines some good practice and some of the common organizational issues concerning planning and evaluation which emerge during assessments.

Finally, we examine how much written evidence is needed, in an attempt to dispel the myth that the assessment (or indeed any part of the process) is about bureaucracy.

Looking at the Standard

The Investors in People Standard (see Appendix 1) is broken down into three elements:

- 4 principles;
- 12 indicators;
- 33 mandatory evidence requirements.

To satisfy an assessor, organizations need to demonstrate that they can satisfy each of the 12 indicators and to do this they need to satisfy all 33 of the evidence requirements.

To simplify the process we have started by arranging the evidence requirements into four groups:

- what the organization needs to demonstrate;
- what top management needs to demonstrate;
- what managers need to demonstrate;
- what people can confirm.

Where representative structures exist (Trade Unions, Works Councils, etc) they would provide a fifth grouping.

Outcomes versus processes

One of the key changes in the current Standard concerns the changed emphasis during the assessment from assessors seeking evidence of *processes*, to seeking evidence of *outcomes*. Investors in People UK define an outcome as 'the result or effect of an event'.

For many assessors seeking outcomes does not mean a major change in the way that they carry out assessments. Investors in People has always been about effectiveness and assessors very quickly learnt that this meant seeking evidence of outcomes rather than merely checking the process existed and was being implemented.

Using the Standard to identify best practice

However, this changed emphasis does not mean that organizations do not need processes; in most cases it will be difficult to demonstrate the outcome without having a process to deliver it and/or back it up (see Chapter 6). We are therefore going to examine typical processes that lead to the required outcomes. They are not in themselves mandatory, but research and experience has shown that they enhance and enable good practice. The Investors in People Standard, historically, was based on good practice. No one disputed this. The change of focus from examining processes to seeking outcomes requires the continued adoption of the good practice. Close examination and application of the Investors in People Standard and indicators, and in particular what the assessor will expect people to confirm (see Chapter 10), reveal what the good practice is expected to deliver.

The good practice generally falls into the following broad headings:

- planning;
- identifying development needs;
- delivering development;
- performance review;
- evaluation.

Effective communication is the thread that links them all together.

However, being able to demonstrate the required outcomes in order to be recognized as an Investor in People also relies more than anything on the effectiveness of management (see Chapter 9).

Definition of development
The Standard frequently refers to the development of people. Development as defined by Investors in People UK as: 'Any activity which develops skills, knowledge or attitude. Activities may range from formal training courses run internally or externally to informal on-the-job training, shadowing or coaching.'

What is required in practice?

The remainder of this chapter examines what is required in practice to deliver the required outcomes; marrying the processes to the evidence requirements from the organization and the top management.

The organization

Investors in People UK define the organization as: 'the body that is working towards the Standard. It can be a subsidiary or a business unit, provided it meets the autonomy guidelines' (see Chapter 7).

Four of the indicators start with the words 'The organization'. However, further examination reveals that there are five evidence requirements that clarify what the organization needs to be able to demonstrate. Note also that four of the five organizational evidence requirements revolve around planning and evaluation. The fifth concerns managers and is dealt with in the next chapter.

The organization needs to demonstrate that it:

- has a plan with clear aims and objectives (indicator 5);
- has clear priorities which link the development of people to its aims and objectives at organization, team and individual level (indicator 6);
- makes sure that managers have the knowledge and skills they need to develop their people (indicator 8);
- can show that people learn and develop effectively (indicator 9);
- can show that the development of people has improved the performance of the organization, teams and individuals (indicator 10).

Planning and rationale

These requirements set the context for the development of both the organization and its people. Investors in People is about developing people to help achieve the organization's goals and targets. It is not about having a large training budget, or always saying 'Yes' to people's training requests. Development should be closely focused on the organizational needs now and into the near future.

Investors in People should be seen as a strategic tool so planning should include developing the broad aims or vision. Increasingly organizations are developing values statements which describe the type of organization they aspire to be. To be an Investor in People organizations should value their people. If a values statement is being developed ideally it should include a statement to show how people are valued and treated.

Previous versions of the Standard required evidence of a written plan or plans. After a lengthy debate it was decided that this would no longer be the case. However, there is a strong case to be made for having written plans to provide focus and direction. Describing plans in writing ensures that everyone is clear what the plans are and makes it easier to share the plans with others. This does not mean that every organization must have detailed plans that analyse every eventuality, but its plans should show clear goals and targets which are as measurable as possible, and the timescale over which they are to be achieved.

Measurable goals and targets provide the base for the monitoring and evaluation of organizational performance, and the importance of this cannot be over-emphasized. Some goals and targets may be hard financial measures; others could be measured in terms of perhaps customer or employee satisfaction or reduced wastage rates. The questions to ask are: 'How will we know we are being successful?', 'What should we be doing to improve?' You may find that a number of people in the organization at all levels come up with different and valuable ideas when the questions are posed this simply.

Increasingly organizations are developing Key Performance Indicators (KPIs) to measure performance. They can be used as a baseline against which future improvements can be measured. Including desired KPIs in plans will lead to improved monitoring and evaluation.

The emphasis of Investors in People is always on 'fitness for purpose', so small organizations would not be expected to produce the depth of analysis and detail appropriate to larger organizations. However, good practice indicates that they would be expected to take a longer-term view even if this only covers 12 months ahead. Larger organizations may have three- or five-year strategies.

Identifying and delivering development needs

Linked to this there should also be a plan that includes a 'people dimension' – identifying the broad skills and knowledge or changed organizational culture needed to achieve the organization's objectives. At the organizational level good practice would include defining quite clearly what people managers would be able to do and ensuring managers have the required skills and knowledge to do it. One way to do this would be to consider the use of management standards (see Chapter 9). Again, good practice dictates that the resources needed (ie time, people, money and facilities) are identified to ensure the planned people dimension is delivered.

The most effective plans also allow for contingencies – sudden changes which may also affect the skills and knowledge required from people, leading to more development, and perhaps resources, to meet any revised targets.

Reviewing and evaluating

Finally, at the end of a set period (at least annually) good practice in reviewing progress and evaluating the investment would lead to the organization taking a global view of what has been learnt and its effect on the organization. Perhaps this would include taking a view on the contribution the development has made to the achievement of organizational goals (after all, that's why it was planned).

The whole area of defining success criteria has become more important as more and more organizations come up for an Investors in People review (re-assessment). If they have not got benchmarks against which to compare their performance how are they going to demonstrate continuing improvement?

What an assessor will look for

Ideally written plans should include aims and objectives for both the organization and the development of people. Plans vary from one organization to another. Many organizations have 'business' plans but schools for example would have school development plans, OFSTED action plans and staff development plans. Some service organizations operate through contracts, and these contracts may provide the basis for plans. The assessor will expect the organization to have taken a global view on what, if any, broad changes in skills or knowledge will be needed if people are to be able to deliver the organizational plans. If plans are not written organizations will need to convince the assessor that they do have clear aims and objectives and linked plans for the development of people.

Plans are important as they start an audit trail, which will demonstrate that training and development has been effective. Aims and objectives are therefore the basis for reviewing progress and for evaluation. The assessor will expect senior people to have a shared view of the overall impact of the investment in people.

Top management

Top management are the most senior people in the organization and most probably responsible for setting the strategic direction for the organization. They may be the owners, directors, senior managers or a combination.

There are three evidence requirements which put the onus on top management to *demonstrate* action. Top management:

- can describe strategies that they have put in place to support the development of people in order to improve the organization's performance (indicator 1);
- can describe strategies that they have put in place to ensure equality of opportunity in the development of people (indicator 4);
- understands the overall costs and benefits of the development of people and its impact on performance (indicator 11).

In addition there is a requirement that development is linked to relevant external qualifications or standards (or both), where appropriate (indicator 9).

Rationale

In larger organizations, in particular, top management will be involved in developing a strategy that guides the planning process. There is an increasing recognition that effective people development strategies and policies can have an impact on the bottom line. This group of evidence requirements reflects the need for top managers, on behalf of the organization, to have effective people development strategies that embrace all employees. Having a strategy implies a commitment to develop people. The strategy will outline how an organization intends to develop its people and how it will resource this. The strategy should include the policy of using relevant external qualifications. The indicators imply the need to ensure that the strategy is implemented and that value for money is assessed. This means that the benefits of developing people should be identified and understood by top management.

What an assessor will look for

The assessor will expect top management to describe the strategies they have introduced to develop people to improve organizational performance. They will expect the strategies to include opportunities for all staff regardless of role, hours worked, gender or ethnicity. They will ask how the strategies have been communicated to staff. They will also expect top management to understand the costs (not just the budget spend) and have taken a view on how activity to develop people has impacted on the organization. Did it achieve what it was planned to achieve? What were the benefits? (eg efficiencies, perhaps time savings, achieving more with the same number of people or perhaps increased effectiveness). Did the cost of the investment represent value for money?

The need to communicate

Although the Investors in People standard does not specifically mention a communication strategy some of the outcomes required will be difficult to achieve without one. Chapter 9 describes what assessors will expect people to be able to confirm. This confirmation requires knowledge and understanding 'at a level appropriate to their role'. Many organizations, in order to meet the requirements, introduce some kind of team briefing structure to cascade messages from top management meetings and encourage feedback from the 'shop floor'. This implies that there needs to be a policy on what messages should be shared and some checking mechanism to ensure they are.

Communicating with representative groups

Representative groups are consulted about the organization's aims and objectives (indicator 5).

Where there are recognized employee representative structures such as trade unions, staff associations, works councils or other employee representative committees, the assessor will check how they are communicated with or informed about the organization's aims, objectives and performance and the provision of relevant development to support this. This is the only evidence requirement that can be omitted if it is not relevant because such structures do not exist.

Common weaknesses

Evaluation is often considered to be the most difficult part of Investors in People. We disagree; evaluation is easy if you know what you want. Evaluation merely asks: 'Did you get it?' This puts the onus back on the quality of planning which is where most of the difficulties with evaluation actually lie.

Lack of clear links to organizational objectives

This is often caused by poorly constructed organizational objectives; eg they are vague and perhaps not Specific, Measurable, Achievable, Realistic and Time-bound (SMART). Sometimes where plans are written all the objectives are not written down. This may be because they may be obvious but are they obvious to all?

Sometimes evidence shows evaluation of the organization's achievements and the outcomes of training and development but fails to make a direct link between the two. Quite often it is very difficult to follow the audit trail between the organizational need, the development action and the outcome. An assessor (and the organization itself) should be able to start at any point on the audit trail and trace the links back and forth.

Not evaluating the outcomes of development

Quite often people describe how they were clear about what they were expected to learn and that a discussion or post-event de-briefings took place to check that they had learnt what was expected. What is often missing is confirmation to illustrate that performance is monitored to check that the new skills or knowledge are being applied and are having the desired effect. Sometimes managers say they are monitoring the effect but staff are unaware of it happening.

Evaluating against aims not objectives

Quite frequently managers and organizations have difficulty evaluating, as they are evaluating against aims rather than object-ives. Aims tend to be broad rather than specific. They are often strategic rather than short term, so they can be time-bound but may require a longer time to be achieved. For example, 'to improve the communication skills of reception staff' is an aim. How will you know when the communication skills have improved? The answer to this question will lead to the objective, which could be 'to improve the reception technique and make callers more welcome' or 'to improve the questioning technique of receptionists to enable them to establish the purpose of the call more quickly'. It will be much easier to evaluate the impact of the development in the latter two examples.

Understanding costs but not benefits

In some organizations it is felt that senior managers understand the costs but not the benefits of training and development actions. This implies that expenditure on training and development has been an 'act of faith' and is bound to have a positive effect on the performance of the organization, especially if it is very successful.

In some organizations, especially larger ones, line managers understand the benefits but senior managers don't, which implies that a method of collating information about the effectiveness of the development is needed and that this information should be fed up to senior managers by line managers. This may imply that a written reporting process is needed, which links us to the next point.

Lacking any written evidence

There are no indicators or evidence requirements that require written evidence. The emphasis is on seeking outcomes which can frequently be described by those interviewed during the assessment process.

However, as noted earlier, research suggests that written plans that include clear aims and objectives are effective and are therefore recommended as good practice. The larger the organization the more difficult it becomes to demonstrate effectiveness without having some written evidence.

As mentioned elsewhere in this book, for a number of years there has been a move to actively discourage the use of portfolios of evidence although some organizations still produce them as they clearly find them beneficial.

Many organizations will have quite a lot of 'naturally occurring' documents that can be used to support the assessment process but our advice is generally to let the assessor ask for it rather than spend time accumulating written material that the assessor may not actually need.

However there is a clear warning here: if there is no written evidence you rely on people saying what happens – something over which you have no control! For many organizations this is not a problem, if they are Investors in People! There are, however, examples where employers (or certain line managers) have attempted to influence what their people say to the assessor. This invariably does not work, as it soon becomes clear to the assessor that some kind of brainwashing has taken place.

The simple answer to the question of whether you need written evidence is that it's up to you! (Again – Investors in People works for you, not you for it.)

Summary

This chapter has examined the purpose and links between indicators associated with the organization and top management. It has described a number of linkages that form trails that assessors will seek to follow. It has also highlighted some of the issues that it will be important to demonstrate to assessors, and illustrated some of the weaknesses concerning evaluation at the organizational level. Finally, it has tried to reassure readers about the volume of written evidence needed to satisfy an assessor – just enough is preferable to too much.

CHAPTER 9

The Role of Managers

This chapter examines the pivotal role of managers if organizations are to achieve Investors in People status. It begins by examining who managers are, how their role is changing, and looks at some potential barriers that may prevent them from effectively delivering their responsibilities. It then describes how this fits in with the Investors in People Standard and how the Standard can offer a framework to help managers and organizations.

This chapter examines the indicators from a management perspective. The following chapter examines the issues from the perspective of the people.

Why have a separate chapter on managers?

In previous versions of the Investors in People Standard only two of the indicators actually mentioned managers. This was deceptive, as organizations undertaking the journey towards Investors in People status and those that have completed it would testify. Line managers have always had the significant part to play in helping an organization to meet the Standard. For examples of this, see the case study section. Later in this chapter we will examine the indicators and evidence requirements where managers will impact.

Alarm bells may ring in organizations (and for many managers) who are just starting the journey that this looks like a great deal of extra work. Experience suggests that additional work is generated only in those organizations where line managers are not effectively fulfilling the people development role they are expected to carry out. So if the signs are that a significant amount of extra work will be needed, then before going any further some consideration may need to be given to evaluating the effectiveness of the people management role within the organization.

The changing role of line managers

These are challenging times for many organizations. For many years increased competition, spiralling costs and a range of other factors conspired to create a fast-moving and fast-changing environment. Before examining the line manager's role within Investors in People it is worth looking at how line managers' roles are changing. During the 1990s two strategies employed by organizations that impacted significantly on the role of the line manager were delayering and decentralization. Whilst this trend has continued, for example in the first months of 2000, BT announced significant cuts at management level, there is some evidence emerging that is leading to some people questioning whether delayering may have gone too far.

Delayering/flattening structures

There are many reasons why this delayering occurred but two factors continue to stand out as major contributors to the development of the situation.

First, the increased use of technology made the gathering and use of management information a far more refined and less labour-intensive process. Managers who had laboured over the analysis of this information found that computers were able to carry out the task in a fraction of the time. Indeed, the sophistication of the activity is such that in many organizations the Tom Peters' view that evaluation is the conversion of hindsight into management information is firmly built into everyday working practices. When organizations looked for areas to seek cost reductions this group of managers were prime candidates.

Secondly, there was, and continues to be, a clearly measurable trend to push more and more responsibility down the line. As people accept this responsibility in theory the need to have as many managers disappears. In some organizations whole strata of managers have disappeared as people have become more 'empowered' and have taken additional responsibility. Those managers that are left theoretically have a completely different role, facilitating and supporting staff rather than policing and managing staff.

As we argue in Chapter 12, this is in line with the process of becoming a learning organization, encouraging and enhancing empowerment, self-management and equity of access to training and development, backed up by evident cost-effectiveness.

Decentralizing the personnel, training and development functions

At the same time that layers of managers disappeared, a number of organizations questioned the need for specialist departments to handle personnel and training matters. As a consequence many personnel and training departments are much leaner than they used to be with line managers carrying out some of the functions they once carried out. Theoretically, line managers always have had many of these training and development responsibilities. Training and development, such as it was, was delivered with varying degrees of success. However, the existence of specialists within the organization frequently led to a number of managers abdicating that particular responsibility in practice.

Although many managers organized training themselves there were many more who asked the training department to set it up. Although the situation is improving, there is still evidence from organizations of all types that this trend continues.

There was also a tendency in a number of organizations for training and development to be 'menu' driven, with managers selecting possibilities from a list of training courses prepared by the training department rather than engaging in an in-depth analysis of what is really needed. Although this practice is changing, there are still many organizations, particularly where a training department or training officer exists, where this still happens.

In addition there was previously a focus on training and development as separate or discrete activities rather than on development or on-the-job learning. An increasing number of organizations developed complementary systems. On-the-job training dealt with skills development, job knowledge and requirements relating to departmental priorities. Appraisal or similar processes played a key role in establishing these training needs. Meanwhile, a central facility dealt with items of corporate importance and those areas such as team building where the skills for delivery could not necessarily be expected to be found within departments. Whilst the strategic plan continues to play the key role in establishing these needs it is clear that there is a need for this type of activity to be coordinated and managed.

The increasing pressure on managers

Many of these changes in theory should have eased the pressure on managers to manage more effectively. However, in practice those managers who are left are increasingly under pressure as they absorb work passed down to them but are unable, or unwilling, to pass work down the next level. Sometimes this may be caused by a lack of training and in some cases they do not like to pass work down to people who are themselves perceived as being under pressure. Consequently, in many organizations, there is often a band of managers who are absorbing work passed down to them which leads to them working excessive hours and taking work home.

The manager's role in changing culture

So it has been established that many organizations and their managers continue to face far-reaching change. The need is also to change the culture of UK organizations to enable them to meet global competition.

Culture is frequently described as 'the way things are done around here'. Organizational culture is created by managers. For example management style will create a culture. If a manager is prescriptive and autocratic that will create one culture. At the other extreme, weak and indecisive managers will create a different culture. Of course these cultures and many more can co-exist within one medium to large organization and these cultures can change over time.

Numerous organizations have examined the Japanese organizational culture. However, on closer examination there is clearly no one single Japanese culture; for example, Toyota is quite different to Nissan.

So how can Investors in People help?

If the culture of an organization is created by managers then managers must lead culture change. Underpinning Investors in People is a framework based on good practice in people management. This however is not always readily seen. Until people actually apply the Standard and its indicators to their own organization it will be difficult for them to appreciate the implicit meaning and the importance of the role and behaviour of line managers. The surveys mentioned in Chapter 4 highlighted the fact that managers and staff often have differing perceptions. Does this mean managers need to behave differently? The answer may often be: Yes! The good practice, if applied, will lead to managers behaving differently and delivering the outcomes required by the Investors in People Standard. Once this happens the culture will change and as can be seen the case study organizations in Part Three, effectiveness will increase. If behaviour and culture change in the right way organizations and their people will begin to seek improved ways of doing things. This ultimately must lead to a type of learning organization (see Chapter 12).

In the remainder of this chapter we focus on the indicators that specifically refer to managers. The implication will be that without managers undertaking their role effectively many evidence requirements will not be satisfied.

Definition of managers

The term manager includes anyone who has responsibility for managing and developing people. It includes everyone from first line managers or supervisors to the most senior person within the organization. In education it will include head teachers, deans of schools, vice chancellors. In professional practice it will include partners.

There is one indicator (indicator 8) and four evidence requirements which specifically mention managers. The evidence requirements are that managers:

- can describe specific actions that they have taken and are currently taking to support the development of people (in order to improve the organization's performance) (indicator 1);
- can describe specific actions that they have taken and are currently taking to ensure equality of opportunity in the development of people (indicator 4);
- at all levels understand what they need to do to support the development of people (indicator 8)
- at all levels can give examples of actions that they have taken and are currently taking to support the development of people (indicator 8).

Rationale

If top management sets the strategy then 'managers' implement it. The purpose of this cluster of evidence requirements is to ensure that they do. Of course top management will be managers too and they will be expected to implement their own strategies with those people who report directly to them. Top management in effect should be role models whose good practice should then be cascaded through line management.

These requirements ensure that the changes needed in terms of skill, knowledge and perhaps attitude of teams and individuals are identified and taken into account by the plans of managers (team leaders, supervisors, etc). They also point to the need for managers to be competent and effective. Managers will demonstrate this competence in managing the development of their staff. These requirements link directly to the requirement to demonstrate effectiveness through evaluation so good practice would lead to plans at the 'team level' with clear aims and objectives linked to needs of the organization.

The process should also include the need to consider the benefits and use of appropriate external qualifications. Achieving qualifications rewards individual achievement. It will also add to an organization's credibility in terms of the customer's views of the skills and knowledge of its staff and by providing an externally benchmarked measure of the organization's 'stock' of competence and capability.

Among the external qualifications an assessor will expect organizations to have considered are National Vocational Qualifications (NVQs), or SVQs in Scotland, as well as appropriate national technical or professional certification.

What an assessor will look for
The assessor will expect managers to describe how they have ensured that the strategies have been communicated to staff and implemented. He or she will seek examples of how managers support the development of staff

Although only one indicator and four evidence requirements refer to managers it is by looking at what people are expected to articulate, as described in the following chapter, that a picture begins to emerge about what support from managers actually means in practice.

Supporting the development of staff as a management activity is crucial to enabling the organization to demonstrate it meets the requirements of the Investors in People Standard by delivering the required outcomes. However, this should not just be seen as action needed for Investors in People; the action is essential if organizations are going to optimize the use of their people in achieving their aims and objectives.

So what should managers be doing?

The broad headings outlined in the previous chapter also constitute good practice for managers in managing the development of people:

- planning;
- identifying development needs;
- delivering development;
- handling performance review;
- evaluating.

Once again communication is the thread that links the good practice together.

Planning – identifying development needs
This involves managers:

- being clear about what the organization needs to achieve;
- being clear about how this impacts on individuals and their team;
- understanding what knowledge and skills are needed to achieve it;
- reviewing what knowledge and skills already exist;
- planning to fill the gap between the two.

It is also essential to ensure that there are sufficient resources for delivery in terms of time, people and money.

Development needs may be identified in a variety of ways. Some organizations have performance management or appraisal processes. Others carry out individual development reviews whilst some may carry out reviews in groups, especially where there are a large number of people doing similar and perhaps repetitive jobs. Whatever method is used it should include an opportunity for people to identify what they feel they need to learn in order to do their job more effectively.

To demonstrate the outcomes required by Investors in People assessors will seek from managers examples of development needs that have been identified through these processes. They will also seek illustrations from managers of how they encourage and involve staff in identifying their own development needs to enable them to do their job. On some occasions this may involve *creating* development opportunities, eg through delegation or projects.

Delivering development

Once development needs have been identified and action planned, managers need to ensure that the action does actually take place. When the pressure is on, development can sometimes suffer, with seemingly immediate items pushing it to the back of the priority queue. Managers must, however, ensure that development is not continually or habitually treated as a lesser priority.

Assessors will seek illustrations of development regardless of whether they are of training or learning activities. They ask managers how they ensure that staff understand what they need to learn from the activity and what they are expected to do as a result.

Good practice would involve managers having an informal discussion with the relevant staff to clarify aims and objectives before the staff undertake any developmental activity. The assessor would also seek illustrations that confirm that throughout the process, line managers offer support and encouragement.

Performance reviews and evaluation

Checking on the planned learning and its impact is an important stage in the development process. This should be done in two stages. The first stage is immediately after the activity, when the manager should check whether the person believes the activity has increased knowledge and skills. Then at a later stage the manager should check if the person has had a chance to apply the knowledge and/ or skills whether he or she is actually using them; and whether any shortfalls in the development activity have been addressed, ie when the people were unable to do what they were expected to do. This may involve on-the-job coaching or further formal training or developmental activity.

Many of the planning processes mentioned above – performance management processes, regular reviews or appraisal – can be used to evaluate previously agreed objectives. Team meetings can also be used to review the effectiveness of group development activities.

Again, to meet the requirements of Investors in People, assessors will seek illustrations that managers actually do this and examples of outcomes of how effective it was.

Communicating

Keeping people informed is an important management role. Many employees prefer to be aware of what is happening or being planned. Good practice therefore suggests that communication should take place to ensure staff understand:

- what the organization is trying to achieve;
- how they can contribute to those achievements either as a team member or individually;
- that the organization is committed to helping all people to learn;
- that they understand the contribution development has made to organizational success;
- that they demonstrably share and celebrate successes.

Assessors will expect managers to give examples of how they have communicated with staff in tandem with the 'messages' they expect staff to have internalized and to be able to articulate when assessors question them.

Barriers

As mentioned earlier, in most organizations it is line managers, especially middle managers, who bear the brunt of the changes that take place. In compiling this book we took the opportunity to ask a range of these managers what factors prevent or hinder them from delivering their responsibilities in this area. Some sample responses are:

- 'Lack of time – too busy.'
- 'It's not the way we do things around here.'
- 'If I train my staff too well I'll lose them.'
- 'I haven't been trained to do it.'
- 'I don't see how it will help me to do my job.'
- 'This is just another management idea that will eventually go away.'

The majority of managers have some sympathy with the notion that 'initiative overload' can (and often does) prevent them from doing their job properly.

Obviously if managers are to take on these responsibilities and discharge them effectively they are going to need persuading that there is something in it for them. They will need a lot of support from their line manager – both moral support and offers of help to deliver and understand what needs to be done and how to do it. If they have not been properly trained to manage, appraise, coach and develop staff this will need to be addressed by the organization as a matter of priority. Managers will need these skills and the organization needs them to have them.

Managers will also need help to deal with the belief that developed staff are more threatening, more challenging and will probably have higher expectations for themselves and of their line manager. Managed, supported and developed properly, however, more able staff can actually make the job of a line manager easier.

In many organizations it is clear that some managers, in spite of work pressures, do develop staff whilst others don't. Why can some find the time whilst others cannot? The answer is usually that they believe there are benefits and are therefore committed to ensuring opportunities are created and taken. The bottom line however is that to ensure that the people are able to convince the assessor managers will need to demonstrate a *commitment* to developing people.

Management qualifications and development

Management qualifications and Investors in People

In 1987, a report produced by Handy, Constable and McCormack entitled *The Making of British Managers* compared the qualifications of British managers with their counterparts in Japan, Germany and the USA. The report showed that British managers were far less qualified. This report led to the creation of a movement which established the Management Charter Initiative (MCI), which initially considered the concept of a 'Chartered Manager' but ended up with a set of management standards that managers should be encouraged to meet. An increasing number of organizations are examining MCI with a view to encouraging their own managers to demonstrate competence against its Management Standards.

In 1993, MCI and Merseyside Training and Enterprise Council undertook an exercise that compared the requirements of the MCI Management Standards and those of the Investors in People Standards. Not surprisingly there was a significant correlation between the two. A number of organizations that have met the Investors in People Standard have also used the MCI Management Standards. This work was updated during 1998 and published in a booklet *Managing Business Success*, available from MCI. (See also Chapter 13).

Management development and Investors in People

Organizations that elect not to consider using the MCI Management Standards or any other management standards or competences will need to check whether their managers are sufficiently trained and developed in terms of skills and knowledge to support and deliver the outcome requirements of Investors in People. There is considerable evidence emanating from the assessment of a number of organizations that initially managers have often failed to demonstrate appropriate competence and/or commitment and those organizations did not therefore meet the Investors in People Standard. Although there are invariably a range of reasons as to why an organization is deemed to be not yet ready for recognition, it is most unlikely that one which has not got demonstrably effective line managers will meet the Investors in People Standard.

Summary

This chapter has examined how the role of the line manager is crucial in helping organizations to meet the Investors in People Standard. It has focused on some current issues and the skills and knowledge requirements of managers in managing and developing staff. These requirements are necessary in promoting a more effective, learning organization and for the achievement of Investors in People status. The next chapter is the acid test as far as managers are concerned. If managers are effective their staff will confirm it. If not . . .

CHAPTER 10

The Acid Test

This chapter follows on from the last two by examining the indicators which, if demonstrated, will confirm whether the organization really is an Investor in People or not. Previous chapters have focused on the views of the organization and its managers and what they believe should be happening. This chapter concerns the views of employees – the people and what they believe is happening.

Who are 'people'?

Investors in People UK defines people as: '(all those) who (help) the organization achieve its objectives – whatever role they play'.

Where an indicator refers to people it refers to everyone in the organization. This includes part-time workers and voluntary workers. It may include self-employed people who do a lot of work for the organization on renewable short-term contracts and regular casual employees.

Defining 'people' is increasingly important with the changing patterns of employment. The simple rule is that if they have a direct impact on the achievement of the organization's objectives they are classed as 'in scope' and therefore are likely to be included in the representative sample. However, it is not always that simple.

Morally and legally at least, employers have responsibility to ensure that anyone working for them under any arrangement has the knowledge to work safely on the premises or site and to carry out the work required.

An organization would not normally be expected to provide development for most self-employed people. Nor would it be expected to provide for those employed by another organization brought in because of their specialist knowledge or expertise, such as college staff who are contracted to teach their particular specialism for perhaps one session a week.

Where some of these people are included an assessor will not always expect complex systems to manage such people – again it's a question of 'fitness for purpose'. However, the assessor may elect to talk briefly to a sample of such people to confirm your explanation.

Is the Standard effective in practice?

It has always been an important part of the assessment process that assessors speak to the people to validate the claims of the organization and its managers. The changes to the Standard maintain the principle that of the 33 evidence requirements, 19 start with the word 'people'. To clarify both the rationale and what the assessors will look for in the 'people requirements' we will use similar headings to those used in the previous chapters:

- communications;
- planning;
- identifying development needs;
- delivering development;
- performance review;
- evaluation.

This time however, we will start with communications.

Communications

The communication processes are, or more critically, *should* be involved in everything that happens within an organization. This cluster of requirements focuses on the wider aspects of communication, which should of course be reinforced through ongoing processes at the individual and team level. People:

- can consistently explain the aims and objectives of the organization at a level appropriate to their role (indicator 5);
- can explain how they contribute to achieving the organization's aims and objectives (indicator 7);
- believe that the organization is genuinely committed to supporting their development (indicator 1);
- confirm that the specific strategies and actions (to support the development of people) described by top management and managers take place and recognize the needs of different groups (indicators 1 and 4);
- can explain the impact of their development on their performance, and the performance of their team and the organization as a whole (indicator 11).
- can give examples of relevant and timely improvements that have been made to development activities (indicator 12).

To meet these evidence requirements effective communications is essential. The requirements are focused on what people believe and understand. The understanding sought is at a level appropriate to a person's role.

Rationale

The function of these requirements is to ensure that all employees are aware of what the organization is trying to achieve and how they can contribute to its success directly and through the enhancement of their skills. As well as being clear about their own role they should be confident that the organization will equip them with the skills and knowledge necessary to carry out their role. As indicated in Chapter 7, the commitment to ensure this happens starts at the top of the organization, by giving an adequate priority to 'business' led (training and) development, alongside other organizational priorities and setting a strategy to support this commitment. The strategy should involve encouraging line managers to demonstrate their own commitment.

This cluster of requirements indicate that people should be aware of the organization's strategy for developing people to reinforce the commitment. Belief in this commitment, however, can be very fragile. It is therefore important people feel that the organization shows a continuing commitment. This involves communicating to them the contribution the development of people has made to organizational successes. This contribution will have been identified through the evaluation processes described in the previous chapters. Such a message implies that the organization will continue to develop people because it pays to do so. It will involve:

- celebrating the successful achievement of business objectives and how development has contributed;
- periodically reinforcing, through communication processes, the benefits achieved from the spend on development;
- individual or team achievement of qualifications or other successes where development has contributed;
- improving processes that support the development of people and if appropriate the delivery of the development.

What an assessor will look for

Assessors will want evidence that people (at all levels) confirm the belief that the organization (ie senior people and all line managers) is committed to their development. They need to establish that people believe there is equality of opportunity for development. They will ask how the senior team demonstrates its commitment – is it only in words or in actions and resources? They will ask the following questions. What are the strategies that the organization has in place to support that commitment? Are people aware of the strategies that have been developed to reinforce the commitment? Are people able to explain, in their own words, what the organization is trying to achieve and how they contribute? Do they believe their contribution is recognized? Can they explain in their own words how it is recognized? Are the descriptions consistent? Do they coincide with what the organization is trying to achieve? Can they explain how development has helped them and the organization to develop? When development is successful are they encouraged to develop further? Are they aware of any developments to improve the development processes or the development activities?

Identifying development needs

People:

- can give examples of how they have been encouraged to improve their own performance (indicator 2);
- can give examples of how they have been encouraged to improve other people's performance (indicator 2);
- clearly understand what their development activities should achieve, both for them and for the organization (indicator 6);
- understand what their manager should be doing to support their development (indicator 8);
- describe how their contribution to the organization is recognized (indicator 3);
- believe that their contribution to the organization is recognized (indicator 3);
- receive appropriate and constructive feedback on a timely and regular basis (indicator 3);
- describe how their managers are effective in supporting their development (indicator 8).

Rationale

These outcomes depend on line managers fulfilling their role as outlined in the previous chapter. To meet these requirements managers will ideally need to have created within their teams a spirit of continuous improvement through teamwork, mutual support and shared learning. Whilst an organization may have decided that managers are responsible for managing the development of employees it does not mean that they have to deliver it all themselves. The role of the manager in this process should be clear to everyone. It may lead to identifying people within the team who are able to take a lead in developing the skills and knowledge of their colleagues. It also requires managers to develop a culture of feedback and recognition so that people feel that their contribution to the team and the organization is recognized and appreciated.

What an assessor will look for

Whereas in the past the assessor would look for processes, he or she will now seek examples of development activity to illustrate the effectiveness of the various identification and planning processes. So assessors will ask for examples of development undertaken (including the use, where relevant, of external qualifications), how and why the need for development was identified, what it was meant to achieve in terms of learning and its application. Investors in People is not about development for development's sake so assessors expect to see how the needs link back to the needs of the organization. They will also seek examples of feedback and recognition. This may be through formal processes such as team meetings, appraisal and reviews but ideally should also be on a continual basis. Assessors will recognize that the need for and the degree of feedback will vary from one person to another but will expect managers to be aware of this. By talking to people assessors can collect a great deal of evidence to confirm that line managers are effective at developing their staff; and that they are demonstrating their competence by identifying development needs and creating the 'learning climate' for their teams in support of the commitment from the organization.

Managers are of course 'people' as well, so assessors need to check that needs of line managers have been identified and seek examples of appropriate management development, feedback and recognition for managers themselves.

Delivering development

People:

- new to the organization, and those new to a job, can confirm that they have received an effective induction (indicator 9);
- give examples of what they have learnt (knowledge, skills and attitude) from development activities (indicator 9).

Rationale

One quite simple question which will be asked is: If development action has been identified as being needed does it actually happen? Also, are new employees introduced effectively to their job, the organization, its environment and systems? Similarly, are those existing employees who change jobs introduced effectively to their new jobs? Do they get any initial training they need? If jobs are expanded do people receive the training and/or development necessary to carry out the additional responsibilities? Are the development needs of new line managers met? Does action take place, in spite of other priorities, to achieve those skills and knowledge areas that were identified as necessary to meet the goals and targets of the business, and the needs of individuals?

Because identified action will not always require a formal training course but training that takes place on the job, the line manager has an essential role in supporting through encouragement and coaching and in providing adequate time and resources. In short, the assessor will expect a similar kind of commitment from line managers that is expected from the top of the organization.

What an assessor will look for
The assessor will look for examples of developmental activity that have taken place to confirm that the identified needs of new and existing employees have been addressed. He or she will want a description from people of what they have learnt from the activity and what managers have actually done to support their development.

Performance reviews and evaluation

People:

- can give examples of what they have learnt (knowledge, skills and attitude) from development activities (indicator 9);
- can explain the impact of their development on their performance, and the performance of their team and the organization as a whole (indicator 11);
- can give examples of relevant and timely improvements that have been made to development activities (indicator 12).

Rationale
The assessor will check the effectiveness of the developmental activities by asking questions such as: Did the activities achieve what was expected? What difference have they made to the performance of individuals and/or teams? Have further developmental needs or improvements been identified? As a great deal of development or learning may be through the job itself, how is this evaluated? How do managers 'manage' the process?

What the assessor will look for

The assessor will be seeking an audit trail that demonstrates effective evaluation of:

the business or organizational need
↓
the learning need
↓
the 'development' action
↓
the learning achieved and
↓
the impact on the business as a whole.

The audit trail may start in one of the following places:

- with the learning objectives set at the identification of development needs (eg at appraisal or whatever other method is used to identify needs);
- at a pre-event briefing or discussion;
- at the start of formal training sessions;
- during on-the-job training, ie with the explanation that sets the context for the training.

Assessors seek illustrations from people of developmental activity undertaken to confirm that they were clear about what they were expected to learn, what they were expected to able to do with the learning and what impact is expected. They will check that the relevant line manager managed this process in the way the organization expected. They will also ask what happens if performance does not improve with questions such as: Is further training or development planned? Was it the activity itself that was at fault? Could the activity be improved?

Summary

This chapter has examined the criteria concerning the views of the people. Are the organization and its managers serious about the development of people or are they merely paying lip service to it? This chapter has examined what evidence the people will be able to supply to the assessor to confirm, or not, that the organization truly is an Investor in People.

PART THREE: THE EXPERIENCES

Introduction to the case studies

The organizations featured here have been selected to illustrate how the various stages in the process were tackled. They were chosen to represent a cross-section of organizations by size, sector, location and management philosophy. Some of them are household names. Others you may not have heard of. Nevertheless, they all have a common purpose: to develop their organization by developing their people.

Most of the organizations featured here have achieved recognition as an Investor in People. As we are discussing a continuous process, we include organizations which were at different stages of their journey towards recognition. This enables the reader to gain an insight into organizational decision-making, action planning and implementation of decisions as they take place.

Case Study I
Amwell View School

The organization

Amwell View School provides education for pupils with very severe learning difficulties (eg autism, multiple physical and sensory impairment). There are currently 83 pupils (ranging in age from 2 to 19) on the school roll, largely drawn from the local area of east Hertfordshire. There are 55 members of staff plus volunteers and supply teachers.

The school is located on the outskirts of Stanstead Abbots, on the Herts/Essex border. Although semi-rural in location, it is well connected to the surrounding area. The staff group includes teachers (including the head and two deputies, all of whom teach in addition to their managerial roles), non-teaching assistants, nursery nurses, music therapists and support staff including a group of midday supervisory assistants. The school is organized into teams in terms of role, but also in terms of task, so that the classrooms are staffed by a team that might well comprise one teacher, one teaching assistant, a midday supervisory assistant (the children have their meals in their small class groups) and volunteers.

Reasons for making the initial commitment

Amwell View School first learned of Investors in People following a meeting with its TEC where the benefits were outlined and discussed. The managers attending found the meeting very helpful and decided to seek recognition. They felt that it would help to improve their systems and processes as in their words, 'we have the procedures but not the systems'. Unlike other schools, special schools have large numbers of additional staff supporting learning in the classroom. The business of teaching and learning was everyone's business and it was important to the school that everyone understood this: 'We wanted to see ourselves as whole teams.' This type of school must clearly be well prepared for any eventuality and most events/crises are one-offs; therefore there is an appropriate focus on preparing staff at all levels – support and teaching – in managing behaviour.

The approach

The School Development Plan forms the main document setting out the school's goals and targets, but it is supported by various others including curriculum schemes of work, statutory teaching assessment and various other reporting and recording requirements.

The plan and its accompanying documentation note the commitment to continuously improve the quality of teaching and learning. It is also important to note that this does not relate only to teaching staff, but acts as an all-embracing agreed set of targets for all to work towards as individuals and members of various teams. There are, of course, the various statutory requirements that necessarily comprise a significant element within the plan and related documents. These include, for example, the Code of Practice for Pupils with Special Educational Needs, the National Curriculum and the Children's Act.

Target setting

Targets and objectives for newly qualified teachers (NQTs), appraisal for teaching staff, review for support staff and individual action plan targets all inform the setting of objectives on the wider organizational level as well as setting them for individuals. The objectives for training and development are clearly set out in the school development plan, which is supported by a staff development policy. Team targets are set in a variety of formal and informal ways, for example with regard to class team training plans. One objective had been to further improve the ability of the midday supervisory assistants to respond to difficult classroom situations, like the administering of rectal Valium. It is interesting to note that this training was done under the heading of INSET, a title most schools reserve for teacher training and development, but here all staff become involved where appropriate and in support of their role. This is entirely in line with the broad objective of inclusion of all staff as described by the school.

Evaluation

The school evaluates the impact of training and development actions in a variety of ways and at a variety of levels. Newly qualified teachers are regularly observed by senior and more experienced staff and their development is discussed and monitored. Curriculum policy documents and class files provide a clear monitored record of progress against objectives – whether they relate to the team, to an individual or specifically to one child.

There is constant evaluation of each child's progress. To plan and deliver effective teaching and learning and concomitant support requires constant evaluation and feedback. This includes many formal measures (appraisal, review, action plans, the OFSTED Report, the school development plan and so on). However, of particular importance to the school is the informal, almost constant evaluation of performance against a child's progress; and the training and development actions that ensue (eg Makaton, autism, IT, management development) are, in essence, actions taken as a result of evaluation.

The benefits

The introduction and embedding of new systems and processes was a key benefit. The development of an induction package for all staff was an additional outcome. Of particular importance was the introduction of a professional development review for the classroom assistant on an individual basis. This enhanced the collegiate nature of the school and enabled performance to be looked at objectively: 'Investors in People has made us much more efficient, it enables us to monitor, evaluate and, importantly, to be reflective.' The school also believes that the process has encouraged a focus on the key activities by all staff.

Communication across the school has improved significantly, including communication with its very active governing body.

Benefits are not only confined to the school's own perceptions. An OFSTED inspection report noted that: 'the inspirational leadership of the Headteacher, who is ably supported by her deputies, underpins the very positive ethos of the school. The . . . progress which pupils and students make is also due to the dedication and care of all the staff.' The OFSTED report also notes that 'involvement in Investors in People has . . . helped focus the management thinking and made a very positive contribution to professional development.'

Key messages

The key message the school offers is 'Don't be discouraged' – the initial diagnosis was a 'painful process'. Staff felt they had much to do to achieve recognition and felt uneasy about the prospect. However, getting people involved early on, making it clear what you are doing and why and emphasizing communication will see you through to reap the benefits later on, the school believes.

Finally it is interesting to note that the school now believes it has strong documentation – its strategic planning processes, its induction material, etc – and that there is no longer separate OFSTED and Investors in People material. 'This is what we are.' The process and its concomitant improvements are now fully assimilated.

Case Study II
Barnsley Magistrates' Court

The organization

Barnsley Magistrates' Court serves Barnsley Metropolitan Borough and is one of four magistrates' courts serving South Yorkshire. The Court is funded by central Government (80 per cent) and the local authority (20 per cent). The funding that comes from central Government is paid by the Lord Chancellor's Department through a cash-limited grant. The cash limit is calculated by using a formula based on performance.

The court is managed by the Magistrates' Court Committee, a body of 12 members selected by a selection panel. The Committee, which is supported in its work by a Justices' Chief Executive, employs 50 staff, eight on the legal side of the business and 42 on administration, finance and support services. In line with many public sector organizations some work, for example court security and cleaning, has been contracted out to the private sector. In addition the court has 124 Justices of the Peace and a Stipendiary Magistrate, who is employed by the Lord Chancellor's Department but based at this court.

Reasons for making the initial commitment

For some time, as part of the Government's drive for efficiencies, effectiveness and accountability in the public sector, the Lord

Chancellor's Department has been examining ways of increasing value for money from the funding of Magistrates' Courts. In South Yorkshire an amalgamation of a number of courts has been anticipated for a number of years. In the past Barnsley Magistrates Court was not recognized as particularly effective and efficient compared with other courts and was well down the performance league table published by the Lord Chancellor's Department. The arrival of a new Justices' Chief Executive presented an opportunity to look at improving performance and morale and to position staff to enable them to compete for jobs should an amalgamation take place.

The Lord Chancellor's Department was encouraging Magistrates Court Committees to develop strategic plans. The approach that Barnsley Magistrates' Court Committee took was to involve all staff in the process as much as possible. A day was put aside during which staff were divided into small working groups to develop a mission statement and gather ideas about the future. Following this day a strategic plan was developed which was presented to staff for comment and then presented to the Magistrates' Court Committee for final approval. During the planning process it was agreed that as far as possible national standards would be used to bring about the required changes. ISO 9000 was chosen for the systems and Investors in People for the staff.

The formal commitment to Investors in People was made in July 1997.

The approach

Shortly after the strategic plan had been agreed a new head of management services was appointed who selected members of a senior management team to manage a change project. This project involved examining and developing the communications, personnel and training processes, and introducing performance management. At this time a diagnostic survey was carried out against the Investors in People Standard, which identified a number of issues:

- communications – the need to develop understanding of how people contributed and how training *and* development fitted in;

- training and development needs – the need for a structured process;
- improved processes to evaluate the effectiveness and impact of training and development on individual and organizational performance.

As a result the existing communications processes were strengthened and formalized. An internal newsletter was developed. Team meetings were encouraged and, in a spirit of increased openness, minutes of meetings were more widely circulated than previously.

Middle managers' roles were enhanced. Some operational tasks previously carried out by senior managers were passed on to middle managers who were now referred to as operational team leaders. Management standards were used to develop these operational team leaders' skills and knowledge and help them carry out their enhanced roles.

An annual staff review and development system with six-monthly interim reviews was introduced for all staff. Training was provided to enable reviewers to carry out their responsibilities and for reviewees to enable them to get the best from the process.

Staff were encouraged to recognize that training was wider than just courses and included a range of development activities; consequently the range and scope of training and development activity were broadened.

Magistrates' training, which is agreed nationally, had always been quite structured but it was not totally immune to the impact of Investors in People, especially in relation to evaluation. However, the need to improve the Court's performance highlighted a number of training issues that affected both staff and magistrates. One in particular, the need to reduce delays in court, brought together magistrates, relevant staff and court users, eg defence solicitors, in a training event. Other activities involved only staff, such as training aimed at reducing costs through improving internal efficiencies.

Finally, processes were introduced to evaluate the effectiveness and impact of training and development. Pre- and post-event discussions were introduced. Training and development became part of the agenda for most management meetings including the Magistrates' Court Committee.

In February 1999 it was felt that they were doing enough to meet the Investors Standard. They applied for assessment and subsequently satisfied the assessor, and the Court was recognized as an Investor in People.

The benefits

The turnaround in performance has been amazing. From being as low as 101st in some performance tables Barnsley Magistrates' Court is now as high as 10th. Delays in its court have been reduced to below the national average. Other performance indicators such as costs per case and debtor days have improved.

Staff morale has improved through increased involvement and better communications and the fact that staff can now hold their heads high when acknowledging they work for Barnsley Magistrates' Court. Middle managers' skills have developed and they also feel more involved in the running of the Court.

A Court Charter has been developed. ISO 9000 has been retained and a positive report was received following an external review by the Magistrates' Courts Inspection team.

The Court and its staff are well placed to be able to compete for jobs when the voluntary amalgamation of the four South Yorkshire Courts takes place from April 2001.

Following recognition, the Court gained two notable firsts – it became the first Magistrates' Court to win an NTA (National Training Award) and the first to gain Beacon Status (Government initiative to recognize good practice in the public sector).

Case Study III
Le Meridien Excelsior
Hotel Heathrow

The organization

Le Meridien Excelsior Hotel is part of Forte Hotels, which in 1997 became a wholly owned subsidiary of Granada Group. It is one of seven hotels that form the London Signature Hotels Strategic Business Unit.

The original hotel was built in 1964 as a 330-bedroom Trust-house Forte Motorlodge named the Excelsior and over the years it has increased in size, reaching 665 rooms in 1972. By 1990 it had 829 rooms, of which 248 were executive rooms, allowing the hotel to be rebranded as a Forte Grand Hotel. The hotel has three restaurants, two bars and the largest conference and banqueting facilities at Heathrow, capable of accommodating up to 700 people. The hotel is now the third largest in the UK, and caters for airline crews, commercial clients, conference delegates and leisure groups. At the time of the assessment the hotel was known as the Excelsior Hotel and employed some 440 people, including casual and agency staff.

Reasons for making the initial commitment

The hotel became aware of Investors in People at the same time as a number of business aims were identified. These included the need to improve customer satisfaction levels and reduce staff turnover, which in turn would lead to increased repeat business. The Investors in People process was seen as complementary to the processes needed to achieve the business aims. The commitment to become an Investor in People was therefore made in October 1995 and renewed in September 1996 when a new general manager took over.

The approach

As in most organizations, communication in the hotel was seen as vital in managing the business. The hotel already had an established structure of meetings involving a series of daily, weekly and monthly meetings. To this was added an AGM for staff. At this meeting the general manager outlined his vision and the objectives and targets for the hotel. These objectives and targets are established through the business planning process. As many staff work shifts the general manager holds the AGM three times to enable all of them to attend.

This strong culture of communication is enhanced by the use of a newsletter, notice boards and a Staff Consultative Committee, which meets every four weeks and has been reconstituted to meet the need for a European Works Council.

To address the need to improve customer satisfaction levels it was decided to develop a customer care programme that all staff would attend. This led to the concept of the Passport to Excellence programme.

This programme involved a series of five two-hour customer care modules. To gain ownership and contribute to reducing staff turnover each participant in the programme was given a 'passport' that was stamped as they attended the modules. The passport included:

- a copy of the Meridien Excelsior's mission and values;
- a place to put a 'smiling' photograph;
- 10 management commitments, signed by the departmental manager;
- a space for the team member to enter and sign up to 'team member commitments';
- space for details of other training to be entered and stamped.

The 10 management commitments include:

- I will seek your opinions and suggestions, and implement feasible ideas.
- I will have an open-door policy ready to listen – help – support.
- I will allow you to make decisions within guidelines.
- I will give you the training and equipment that will enable you to do your job with confidence.
- I will review your development every six months and give you feedback.
- I will inform you of business plans and performance for the company, the hotel and the department.
- I will smile.

Another contribution to reducing staff turnover was the introduction of 'personal learning logs' for every employee. These also included a copy of the mission statement, along with the employee's job description and a personal development plan. The personal development plans were drawn up during a new appraisal process. This involved six-monthly appraisals and regular 'job chats' during which the personal development plans would be updated. Senior managers took part in a 360 degree appraisal process. All new employees are given a passport and personal learning log as part of their induction and have a job chat within four weeks of starting.

The benefits

The Passport to Excellence programme was completed over a two-year period. The programme made a significant contribution to meeting the original aims of improving customer satisfaction and reducing staff turnover.

Customer satisfaction is measured in a number of ways: mystery guest reports, customer monitoring and the level of complaints. All have shown improvement. Clearly a good measure of improved customer satisfaction concerns the level of repeat business and this increased significantly. Qualitative feedback from a major client also confirmed the improvement in customer satisfaction: this client commented that in 1995 it only used the Meridien Excelsior as a last resort – now the Meridien Excelsior is the client's first choice hotel at Heathrow.

In early 1997 the hotel was assessed and recognized as an Investor in People. An additional benefit, including significant publicity, occurred at the end of 1997 when the hotel won an NTA for its Passport to Excellence programme.

Recent developments

The hotel has undergone a number of changes since it was recognized in 1997. As well as being re-branded as a Meridien Hotel it lost a major contract with BA who opened their own hotel nearby. This led to a re-structuring and alterations with a number of redundancies following a reduction in bedrooms. The hotel also went through a programme of 'Meridienization' with the introduction of a 5-star service.

HR practices have been strengthened with the introduction of:

- NVQ-linked job descriptions;
- modern apprentices;
- improved succession planning;
- new-style induction programmes.

The hotel came forward for an Investors in People review in January 2000 when it was re-recognized as an Investor in People.

Case Study IV
HPC Industrial Products Ltd

The organization

HPC was founded in 1960 in St Albans. Initially the organization sold all forms of packaging, including self-adhesive tapes, corrugated cardboard and string. A close working relationship developed between HPC and 3M UK Ltd (now 3M UK plc). From 1965 the emphasis moved more and more to the distribution of the Scotch range of speciality tapes. HPC became a preferred dealer and moved to Welwyn in 1977. Expansion and diversification lead to a Basildon office being opened in 1984. The Welwyn and Basildon branches were combined in 1992 and relocated to Pin Green Industrial Area, Stevenage. Today the organization stocks a wide range of self-adhesive tapes and adhesives and has its own tape printing and slitting facilities. HPC achieved ISO 9002 in July 1994 and was recognized as an Investor in People in 1996. The organization is a privately owned company and employs 20 people, over half of whom are dedicated to sales and sales support.

Evaluation

HPC has a written business plan, setting out goals and targets. The company devises and implements its training plan, reviewing and changing it on a regular basis.

HPC's array of evaluation instruments is impressive – particularly considering the organization's size. A combination of board meetings; business opportunity reviews that culminate in a document circulated to all staff; reviews of training goals and a measurement form (HPC 141); and appraisals, measure impact at all appropriate stages. The Board Meetings operate a continuous system of monitoring and review. (An example form performing similar functions to the HPC 141 can be found in *Managing for Investors in People* (2001) by the authors of this book, also published by Kogan Page.)

HPC evaluate the impact of training and development actions at several levels. They know if people enjoyed the activity (HPC 141), whether they learnt anything (HPC 141, line manager review), whether the learning is being applied (follow-ups, line manager observation, appraisal) and what the impact has been on the organization (appraisal, strategy meetings).

Examples include, at the individual level, a warehouseman who worked out his own objectives (and has them reviewed over time) in consultation with the warehouse supervisor and the operations director. A sales representative identified the need to convert more telephone calls to appointments. This need was met by 'dual working' with an experienced colleague and by attending an external course. An analysis of telephone call conversions was conducted before and after. With a further analysis later, improvement – and evidence of it – was monitored and sustained.

HPC spends 4.5 per cent of its budget on training and development. A specific element (1.8 per cent) is allocated for external programmes and activities and all staff are aware of what investment has been made in them by informal means (eg copies of memos or letters) and by inclusion of cost on their HPC 141s. (This has been enhanced, developed and widely circulated since its inception seven years ago.)

Academy of Chief Executives

The three directors of HPC belong to the Academy of Chief Executives. This is a group of senior staff in the region from non-competitive companies. It meets once a month and serves as a support network.

Business and personal goals are discussed and reviewed and there is normally a speaker on a topic of shared interest. The activity lends some considerable support to the in-house appraisal of senior staff as well as providing excellent development opportunities.

The benefits

HPC has noted a significant increase in staff commitment since beginning the Investors in People process.

There is now a meaningful structured appraisal for all staff, which serves as 'a start for everything else'. This includes objective-setting at the individual level, with these objectives being drawn from the corporate objectives, thus enhancing all the staff's understanding of their function and purpose.

Since recognition, HPC has worked very closely with its local TEC and has found this very beneficial, with, for example, a range of funding opportunities being successfully pursued in partnership with the TEC.

Key messages

Organizations definitely need a champion, and it shouldn't be the managing director. It is essential that action plans drawn up in the early stages are produced via consultation with all staff at all levels and do not suddenly appear via an external consultant. Ownership at this stage is vital.

Once an organization gets the initial processes in place, upkeep is relatively simple – a robust system should maintain itself – but that 'champion' will always be needed to keep things moving on and to take the lead on issues such as evaluation.

Case Study V
Powerminster Limited

The organization

Powerminster Limited, based in Sheffield, is a member of the M J Gleeson Group of Companies. The company's experience as a building services engineering and maintenance contractor has been built up over a number of years. It is recognized as a leader in 'quality contracting' focusing on customers' needs. Its business philosophy is to provide its customers with 'engineering quality and service' through a broad-based, flexible organization. It provides a single source of supply through a multi-disciplined service. Its business is focused on:

- mechanical contracting;
- electrical contracting;
- manufacturing and assembling;
- providing installation, maintenance and 24-hour emergency services.

Powerminster employs over 220 people, a large proportion of whom work on sites throughout the country on a mixture of short- and long-term contracts.

Reasons for making the initial commitment

The managing director saw that Investors in People provided the ideal vehicle for a journey of company and employee development. He felt that adopting the Standard would ensure:

- good quality training;
- improved job satisfaction;
- better communications;
- skill/career development opportunities;
- increased responsibility and involvement;
- a better working environment.

The approach

For Powerminster the journey started in December 1993 with a commitment to work towards the Investors in People Standard. The main recommendations following a diagnostic survey were that the company needed:

- better business planning;
- development of training plans;
- improved communications.

During 1994 the company developed some of the basic planning and communications infrastructure such as:

- launching a company newsletter;
- introducing monthly management meetings;
- developing the business planning process with clear business objectives and success criteria;
- developing job descriptions;
- introducing team meetings;
- introducing NVQ training.

The above developments were consolidated during 1995, as was the development of performance criteria and the 1995–96 budget by managers.

During 1996 the journey took the company along the following route:

- a long-range/strategic business plan was developed;
- team business planning was developed;
- annual performance appraisals were introduced;

- a communications group was developed which revived the newsletter, which had fallen into disuse during 1995;
- induction procedures were improved.

In 1997 the concept of empowerment was introduced. This involved:

- a series of awareness workshops;
- developing a delegated authority matrix;
- establishing the principle of five Business Pillars;
- improving business and training planning;
- developing structured team meetings;
- setting up an Employee Consultation Group;
- starting a programme of management development and supervisor's workshops;
- extending performance appraisal.

In 1998 the final stages of the journey to the milestone of recognition as an Investor in People in early 1999 involved:

- a series of technical development workshops;
- the introduction of a team business planning workbook;
- performance appraisals being extended to supervisors;
- the development of key performance indicators, which were shared with all employees through Team Task talks;
- the introduction of a team skills matrix.

The benefits

Investors in People has enabled the company to achieve controlled expansion with decreasing fixed costs. Between 1994 and 1998 turnover doubled, with an increase in targeted profitability. In addition the company has established:

- self-controlled teams;
- benchmark expertise;
- niche market partnering status;
- a training culture;
- communications links up and down the company.

The future

The achievement of Investors in People status is viewed as a stage in the company's growth. Already it is making plans for further continued improvement through the review by senior management of many of the processes and systems that have been introduced. The feedback from the assessor at the end of the assessment has been noted and will be implemented.

The user-friendliness of Key Performance Indicators are being reviewed through a series of focus groups which will lead to an improved understanding of the business and increased commitment from an already committed workforce.

Case Study VI
Queen Elizabeth's
Boys School

The organization

Queen Elizabeth's Boys School was established in 1573 and has been a fully functional school for over 400 years. The original site of the school was in Wood Street, Barnet, and it moved during the 1930s to larger premises at its current location in Queen's Road, Barnet. The school provides for some 1,150 pupils in the age range 12 to 18.

A former grant-maintained school, Queen Elizabeth's Boys School is now a Foundation School. Legal responsibility for the school lies with the governing body, while responsibility for the daily management of the school lies with the headmaster.

There is a senior management team comprising 10 senior staff who act as coaching leaders to over 70 full-time teachers who make up the teaching staff. There are some 30 support staff who work for the school in administrative, cleaning, catering or site/buildings capacity. The school is heavily oversubscribed and is ranked by OFSTED as being among the top 10 per cent of maintained schools in the public examination league tables. The section on benefits below draws, appropriately, on the OFSTED report. In addition the school has a strong tradition of achievements in sport and music. The school mission is to produce boys who are 'confident, able and responsible'.

Evaluation of training and development

The school has a record of staff training providing a catalogue of all training undertaken since 1989 (the year it became grant maintained). The investment in training and development is controlled by the senior tutor, who ensures that suggested development activities are in line with agreed targets and priorities. One of the clearest measures of performance improvement as an outcome of investment in training and development is the school's examination results. These have improved markedly since 1989. The school is now in the top 10 maintained boys' schools as well as being in the top 10 comprehensives in the country.

The school has a clear training plan; skills gaps are identified and measures are taken to close these gaps. The channel for these measures is the TKON system and, currently, the termly review with support staff. The TKON system is the measure used by the organization to evaluate its development actions. The headmaster is 'the anchor' of the system and all reports go to him. This is followed by analysis and further recommendations at Cabinet, the senior staff team meeting.

Appraisal

TKON is the school's own organizational target-setting and review mechanism, and comprises individual and group meetings with staff based upon individuals' contribution to the school's mission. Goals are set, progressed and assessed in terms of the mission. Although the system originally related to academic staff only, the school, following review of the current system for support staff and as part of their commitment to continuous improvement, is establishing this as the system for all staff. The term is therefore not an acronym, rather it is part of the language 'currency' of the school.

Objectives

An example demonstrating that development actions had achieved their objectives can be seen in the school's IT strategy. The objective was to improve efficiency via the introduction of the SIMS communication software. The school now holds a SIMS site of excellence certificate and joins a small group of schools that have achieved this level of performance with the administrative software.

Training outcomes for individuals are assessed at TKON level and at department level. The senior tutor acts as a monitor of all training applications and related expenditure. These applications also have to be endorsed by the department or subject heads and by the deputy head responsible for staffing. Examination results and applications for places are the key organizational level indicators. The boys are seen by staff as an excellent indicator as to the effectiveness of their own training and development.

The governing body regularly receives reports on the costs and benefits of the development process. The senior tutor is a regular guest at governors' meetings (as are most other senior staff and Cabinet members). The headmaster has a formal target-setting meeting with the chair of the governors and regular reviews are held throughout the year. Proposals and costings of training are a matter of regular discussion. Managers are now expected to draft departmental development plans that enhance performance in relation to the school's mission. The first question on the staff development programme application form asks how the programme relates to the school mission.

The principal performance criteria (exam results, applications, the annual record of achievement and the size of the sixth form are systematically relayed to staff through a variety of measures, both formal and informal. Formally, this is done through the weekly briefing (written and verbal), TKON/departmental follow-ups, and governors' meetings (there are two staff governors and it is custom and practice for other staff to sit in on meetings).

The benefits

There have been many external benefits, notably the NTA and resulting Supreme Winner status and the acquisition of a grant from the National Grid for Learning (which contributed significantly to IT development). Overall, the benefits of Investors in People can, in the opinion of the school, best be summed up by the OFSTED report, excerpts of which are quoted below:

The school meets its mission of producing young men who are confident, able and responsible. . . The school is successful in helping boys reach high standards of achievement in all areas of their lives. . . This is a harmonious school. The pupils are good listeners and respect the views of others. Boys from different backgrounds work well together and learn from each other's beliefs. Pupils feel safe in sharing personal experiences and beliefs and are not afraid to be challenged or challenge others as constructive arguments take place in a respectful and tolerant environment. . . Pupils and staff value each other and feel valued. . . An outstanding feature is the very high standard of teaching which produces exceptional public examination results – compared with other schools, overall standards of teaching in all subjects are most often outstanding. . .

Classroom management is of a very high standard. . . Target setting to help future improvement of work is developing very well. . . The attitude of the boys is of an excellent standard. . . Behaviour in all areas of the school is excellent. . . The provision for social development is excellent. . . Work experience is well supported by excellent careers education.

The school goes from success to success. A group of 50 sixth-formers won the National and All-European Young Enterprise competitions. The publication of the school performance tables in August 2000 showed Queen Elizabeth's Boys School performing excellently with an average 'A level' point score per student of 29.7 against a national average of 18.5, outperforming many fee-paying schools.

Case Study VII
Ronseal Limited

The organization

Ronseal's roots go back to the 1920s when the company was established in Brighton as Ronul Ltd. In the 1960s, it became part of the Izal Group and moved to its present site in Sheffield. Since then it has changed ownership on a number of occasions and since 1997 has been owned by a US company, Sherwin-Williams, one of the largest paint companies in the world.

The company manufactures a wide range of woodcare and waterproofing products for the UK and export markets. It currently employs 220 people on the site in Sheffield and 20 people in a sales and distribution office in Dublin.

Reasons for making the initial commitment

When members of the management team looked at Investors in People they felt that it offered a good structure to help develop the business. Although they felt they were already doing quite a lot of the things needed to meet the Investors in People Standard, many of them were being done informally.

The approach

They agreed to have a diagnostic exercise carried out to find out if their systems were as robust as they believed. Overall the results from the diagnosis were quite positive, although there were a number of areas that could be strengthened:

- people felt reasonably well informed about the company's future plans and how their role helped to achieve them;
- while training needs were identified, the process lacked structure in a number of areas;
- the planning of training and development lacked coordination which led to weaknesses in the area of evaluating outcomes and the impact on performance;
- people were positive about the support they received from managers and supervisors;
- when training needs were identified they were usually met.

As a result of this exercise the company decided to develop a plan to address the weaker areas and in July 1997 they wrote to Sheffield TEC formally declaring their commitment to work towards the Investors in People criteria.

Invitations were sent out for volunteers to sit on an Investors in People Steering Group that would meet bi-monthly. The Group's role would be to advise, guide and assist in the implementation process. Fourteen people volunteered to become involved. During the following 12 months a number of actions took place:

- Existing processes were reviewed and improved where necessary.
- A more structured system of identifying training and development needs was introduced on the shop floor.
- A series of workshops took place for managers and supervisors to ensure they understood their role in supporting Investors in People.
- The planning of training and development was improved and linkages to the business needs made more explicit.
- Existing evaluation processes were strengthened and where necessary new processes were introduced to identify the impact of training and development.

In November 1998 the company was formally assessed and satisfied the assessor that it met the Investors in People Standard.

The benefits

Investors in People became the umbrella bringing together, giving structure to and improving the consistency of a lot of informal processes that existed within the company. The main benefits have been:

- Investors in People has been seen as a vehicle by which management have demonstrated their commitment to the employees.
- It has allowed people to participate, become involved and make a bigger contribution to the business.
- Processes have been standardized and improved.
- It has, and will, contribute to continuous improvement initiatives.
- Management is more aware of the contribution training and development makes to business improvement.

Case Study VIII
The Royce Consultancy

The organization

The Royce Consultancy (Royce) was originally formed in 1979. Initially recruiting for the fast-moving consumer goods (FMCG) and technical sales markets, Royce's earliest clients included Olivetti and Mars. For almost 15 of its 20-year history Royce was a small lifestyle company known for the quality of its recruitment in a niche market.

Latterly Royce have recruited almost exclusively for the pharmaceutical and healthcare markets in the UK and are currently recognized as 'specialists in healthcare resourcing'. With an impressive client portfolio which includes the country's top 20 pharmaceutical companies, and a well-established brand, Royce have enjoyed significant business success and more recently substantial growth. In July 1998, Royce recruited their first managed sales team of 66, including a sales director and six area sales managers on behalf of a major pharmaceutical client.

Operating from a head office in Edinburgh, Royce have a network of regional offices throughout the UK – in Edinburgh, Glasgow, Knutsford, Leamington Spa and Kingston-upon-Thames. This regional distribution of offices represents one of Royce's unique selling points in a highly competitive market, offering clients quality interview and meeting facilities locally, with a high-calibre team of consultants and administrative staff who understand and are responsive to local issues of recruitment.

Reasons for making the initial commitment

As a company, Royce had always invested heavily in the training and development of its people, particularly through coaching and mentoring. However, in line with a strategy of managed growth, Royce recognized that its ambitious plans for expansion would call for a well-structured approach to duplicating the success throughout the UK of its first office. It would also need more formal systems to create the infrastructure and capability required to achieve their business goals.

Having already explored BS 5750 and ISO 9000, Royce was keen to adopt an approach for improving its business performance and capability by bringing its business processes in line with a nationally recognized model of 'best practice'. The Investors in People National Standard underpinned a fundamental belief within the company that its business success would only ever be as good as the people who made it possible.

Royce saw Investors in People as a vehicle that would allow it to formalize existing good practice and improve processes where necessary in order to provide the company with a stable platform for growth. Achieving recognition would communicate the company's ongoing commitment to its clients and staff, thereby enhancing its ability to recruit and retain high-calibre people.

The approach

The first step for Royce was to undertake an organizational audit in the summer of 1997, assessing how close it was to meeting the Investors in People National Standard. This highlighted the business processes that needed to be improved, so an action plan was drawn up identifying the activities necessary to achieve the improvement.

The company's operations manager, Fiona Selalmas, was appointed as Investors in People Champion and project manager internally. This move was seen as critical to the success of Royce's journey, as it maintained the momentum throughout the project and prevented any loss of focus during a very busy period of growth.

Many of the business processes already existed within the company, but needed to be made more formal and explicit internally.

Typically these included formal job descriptions, induction programmes and performance appraisals.

Royce made a formal commitment to Investors in People on 15
December 1997. During the 12 months that followed, Royce
allowed their new formalized processes time to become embedded
while they prepared the company's portfolio of evidence for sub-
mission to the assessor.

The assessment process took two days and involved interviews
with 27 people, representing a cross-section of the company's 105
staff from all divisions across the country. The interviewing method
was a combination of face-to-face interviews individually, with
groups of up to three staff at a time, and by telephone conference
calls for field-based staff.

In Royce's case the assessor was satisfied that the company met
all of the requirements and it was formally recognized as an Investor
in People on 4 December 1998.

The benefits

Royce believe that the attitude of its staff is critical in all aspects
of its business and any company which is considering making the
same journey should be aware of the importance of having commitment to the programme at all levels throughout the organization.
This commitment by staff at Royce was demonstrated during the
assessment process and acknowledged in the assessor's report when
she commented that she had been 'overwhelmed with the positive
attitude of staff towards the company and their pride in working
for such a reputable company'.

There were direct bottom-line benefits too. One of the company's
stated business objectives in the summer of 1997 was to increase
the overall number of placements within client companies. This
business objective was cascaded down through the teams to individuals and training was provided to support them in achieving
their contribution. A subsequent review of the training demonstrated that it had not achieved its aim in terms of contributing to
the business objective. The focus was then shifted to providing
internal workshops and coaching for individuals and this resulted
in Royce achieving its stated business objective – the number of

consultants achieving their target rose from 38 per cent to 55 per cent as a direct result.

Following the recognition ceremony Royce prepared for the next stage of the journey – by drawing up an action plan based upon the assessor's report to ensure that the momentum behind their programme of improvement is maintained.

Case Study IX
Facilities Directorate, Sheffield Hallam University

The organization

This case study is not about a university *per se*, rather it reflects the experiences of an autonomous unit performing functions and services that are typically found in many large organizations. The Facilities Directorate provides support and infrastructure services to the university. It was formed in late 1994 following a review process when the option of outsourcing was being examined for a number of non-core activities within the university. The decision was taken to 'resource rather than outsource'. Before the review, the 12 support services were provided by several departments with separate management reporting lines and little communication. Following the review the support services, together with staff from Business Services and Estates Departments, were brought together to form the Directorate.

The Directorate is led by a facilities director, a deputy and two heads of department. It employs some 600 people on five sites carrying out duties such as catering, security, estate management and maintenance, accommodation services, etc. In addition to providing services the Directorate generates income through a number of business and commercial activities.

Reasons for making the initial commitment

The formation of the Directorate brought with it the need to restructure. In addition, although the university had made the decision not to outsource, there was a need to ensure that the Directorate improved its financial performance so that costs and efficiency would not cause the decision to be reversed. This meant that the workforce had to be equipped to take on the new challenges. Investors in People seemed to offer a structured framework to enable the Directorate to achieve these aims.

The university decided that each school and department should make separate commitments to work towards recognition as an Investor in People. In March 1995 the facilities director made the formal commitment on behalf of the Directorate.

The approach

The diagnostic survey carried out identified that strong focus was needed on improving the effectiveness of communications. It also highlighted that although the Directorate had a business plan, there was a need to link training and development of staff more closely to the business objectives. There were also some issues about the involvement of managers in supporting training and development and a few processes that needed developing.

A communications structure was developed using a team-briefing process, known as Team Talk, to pass on messages and give feedback to the workforce. The director also took every opportunity to speak to employees and this culminated in producing an annual report, which was directed at both the university and the workforce. He also introduced an AGM to which all stakeholders, including the workforce, were invited.

Another key stage in winning over a sceptical workforce was to introduce a personal development programme aimed mainly at the large number of manual workers in the Directorate. It was felt that many of this group of people had been away from education for a long time and had lost the desire to learn and improve themselves. In August 1995 the scheme, called Jumpstart, was launched and in its first year attracted 16 per cent of the potential population. Since then its popularity has increased as people have recognized the value of the scheme.

The new Directorate needed managers to act in a different and more businesslike way. All managers had gone through an assessment centre in order to confirm their posts. The analysis of the assessments revealed a number of training needs which were addressed by a 12-module general management programme devised with an external provider. In addition supervisory staff were trained to a Craft Trainers Award standard to enable them to support and improve on-the-job training.

While all this activity was taking place the supporting systems were being developed. A Staff Development Review Scheme was introduced to identify the training needs of all employees. Skills audits were carried out in some teams and other needs emerged from operational reviews. Training plans were developed and implemented. A Training and Development Service for the Directorate was introduced. A team of three staff was appointed to set up the service and a suite of rooms made available to form a Training Resource Centre.

The Directorate introduced the use of targets and objectives to manage overall performance. Key Performance Indicators were identified to monitor performance and support periodic management reports. Service Level Agreements were set up with the Directorate's main customers. This activity provided information against which the Directorate could benchmark its performance both internally and externally.

A number of formal evaluation processes were also introduced to evaluate the effectiveness of training. These included post-course questionnaires, follow-up after three months and the use of the Staff Development Review Scheme. An annual report was prepared by the Training and Development Service bringing together the results of the evaluations so that senior management was aware of the costs and benefits of investing in people.

In June 1997 the Directorate came forward for assessment against the Investors in People National Standard. The assessor was satisfied that the criteria were met and the Directorate was formally recognized as an Investor in People.

The benefits

The performance of the Directorate has been benchmarked continually and has shown it to compare very favourably with counterparts in other similar establishments, including some outsourced facilities directorates. It is constantly in the upper quartile in published results. The efficient management of the university estate and income generation have contributed to a reduction in budget.

The Jumpstart scheme has been extended to the rest of the university. A number of individuals have progressed as a result of involvement in the scheme. One person has progressed via A levels to undertaking a degree as a result of Jumpstart.

The Annual Report for 1997–98 highlighted the achievements:

- 87 per cent of staff undertook training;
- 22 per cent were accredited courses such as Health and Safety, Craft Trainer, NVQ;
- 73 people participated in Jumpstart;
- £145k was spent on training (the equivalent of £375 per full-time equivalent).

Several changes were made following the first recognition including the introduction of a new training and development manager. A wide programme of NVQs has been introduced along with Learning for Life Portfolios for all the Directorate's staff. The staff induction process has been refined as has the whole business planning process. The organization is self-assessing against the EFQM model.

The Directorate was re-assessed in February 2000 and received a very positive feedback report.

Case study X
Soluna Travel

The organization

Soluna Travel is a retail travel agent with seven branches in Sheffield and Chesterfield. It was established in Oldham in 1960, but when the present owners took it over in 1979 and opened a branch in Chesterfield in 1981, they decided to concentrate the business on the eastern side of the Pennines. The company currently employs 35 people.

Reasons for making the initial commitment

The progression to making the commitment to become an Investor in People followed the company's involvement in a series of activities that started with the managing director, Barbara Neale, deciding to attend a management development course run by Dale Carnegie. Although she had been a manager for many years, she had never had any management training. The course completely changed her views on the way that the business should be managed. This change resulted in her increasing the involvement of her staff in making decisions and encouraging ideas to come up rather than being imposed from the top. She followed up this course with involvement in North Derbyshire TEC's Skills for Small Business programme and the Accelerated Business Development Course by Nottingham Business School. By the time she learnt about Investors in People Barbara felt the company was already doing most of what was required for recognition anyway.

The approach

Barbara wanted to develop customer service and differentiate Soluna Travel from other travel agents. She decided she needed to involve her staff more. To do this she felt she needed to be more open and feed back more information about the performance of the business. She therefore decided to share the business plan with all staff, not just her managers. Weekly feedback was introduced on the previous week's performance. For some time she had established a relationship with travel companies in a completely different part of the country. This relationship involved sharing information about their respective business's performance to enable each other to benchmark their own performance. This was discussed at monthly management meetings but also shared with staff. Internal communication was further enhanced by the introduction of an internal e-mail system.

The diagnostic survey highlighted the need to introduce a system that would involve people in identifying their training and development needs. Barbara had experienced appraisal in previous roles and was determined that any system that was introduced would concentrate more on the future than on the past. With the help of consultants from Dale Carnegie, a personal development review system was designed which also led to every member of staff having a personal development plan.

A number of managers from Soluna Travel have subsequently attended Dale Carnegie courses and this too has contributed to the changed culture within the company.

Evaluating the impact of training and development had been previously attempted but with Investors in People it was developed further. For example, following training events that focused on particular products, the sales of that product are 'tracked' so that the impact of the training on sales can be assessed very closely. Where in the past it had been *felt* that sales had been increased, now it could be demonstrated with a precise figure.

The benefits

Many benefits have resulted. Following the introduction of the personal development reviews many training and development ideas have emerged. The volume of training activity and willingness of people to be involved have grown. The skills training has led to a better approach to selling. Confidence in selling speciality holidays has increased following product knowledge training. Managers feel more involved and the flow of ideas from staff has increased and is used much more than before. This has led to improved company performance. 1998 was the company's best ever year with 20 per cent growth and increased profitability.

In October 1998 Soluna Travel became one of only a handful of travel companies to gain recognition as an Investor in People. Since then the company has gone on to win a number of prestigious awards for the quality of their training:

- an NTA sponsored by DfEE;
- the year 2000 award from the travel industry;
- the TTG travel enterprise – an international award in which they saw off many household names including Disney World.

The company has also continued to develop its staff and refine its processes including the development of a process to collate information about individual staff training and its impact on the business, which makes annual evaluation much simpler. Staff development has also resulted in two staff being promoted to branch manager.

Soluna Travel was re-assessed during 2000 and needless to say succeeded in maintaining its recognition as an Investor in People.

Case Study XI
The University of
Strathclyde

The organization

The University of Strathclyde in Glasgow is the third largest of Scotland's 13 universities. The university's roots lie in the Scottish Enlightenment of the late 18th century. Recent years have seen Strathclyde preserve its traditional strength in science and technology. The university teaches more engineering students than any other Scottish university and has an internationally known business school. The quality of academic activity has been enriched by growing expertise in the arts and social sciences and the merger in 1993 with Jordanhill College, becoming the university's Faculty of Education, served as a platform for new educational developments. Strathclyde believes it is distinctive from other Scottish universities and defines this distinctiveness in its own terms as 'a place of useful learning'. This, the university believes, derives from the high quality of its academic activity and its strength of commitment to the non-academic community. The university operates two campuses – the John Anderson in Glasgow's city centre and the Jordanhill, a parkland campus four miles to the west of the city. The university presently teaches over 17,000 students to degree and postgraduate degree level with a further 37,000 registered on some form of continuing education programme. It employs around 3,400 staff and generates an income approaching £140 million per annum.

The mission

The university has a threefold mission:

- To provide students with the knowledge, skills and confidence which equip them to contribute positively to society.
- To undertake research which combines excellence with relevance and so advances the well-being of the national and international community.
- To promote breadth of educational opportunity, encouraging the personal development of students, of staff and of the wider community.

In responding to the third part of its mission the university will support staff's educational needs, which may not be job specific, as well as their job-specific or vocational needs. As this in turn supports its mission, the university believes this sits comfortably within the Investors in People standard.

Reasons for making the initial commitment

The university made its commitment to Investors in People by letter from the principal to the chief executive of the Glasgow Development Agency on 24 January 1994. The university underwent a mock assessment in May 1997, and a quality audit by the Quality Assurance Agency for Higher Education in July 1998, which recommended a significant number of points relevant to the Investors in People indicators.

The university describes its reasons for seeking Investors in People as follows: it is a 'place of useful learning' and the furtherance of personal development is central to its purpose. Investors in People is a process through which a greater degree of alignment between the university's objectives and those of all its staff can be achieved.

The university wishes to demonstrate to all its staff and to the public at large that it operates to a national quality standard for the development and training of staff which is inclusive in nature and is recognized beyond the higher education sector.

The benefits

The university believes it has gained much from pursuing Investors in People. The main benefits as it perceives them include the following:

- The process taught the university that 'seeking the views of all staff on what it is like to work at the University of Strathclyde can be a somewhat daunting but ultimately rewarding experience!'
- The university discovered the power of a planning process which is designed 'to better inform all staff about what the university is trying to achieve strategically; invites them to align their individual and team contributions with these strategies and then to think through the implications that these will have for their own personal development'.
- The university has 'very significantly increased the attention (it pays) to the needs of support staff such as secretarial, technical and ancillary workers who account in numerical terms for half of the workforce. One aspect of this has been to increase the coverage of (its) formal appraisal processes from 50 per cent to 100 per cent'.
- The university has deliberately maintained its practice of rotating headships in academic departments but states: 'we have very significantly increased the training and development support we offer to heads before they take up their appointment and throughout their headship'.
- Informal induction arrangements for new members of staff have been replaced and significantly improved by the adoption throughout the university of a programme in which the responsibilities of individuals, the departments and the centres are clearly defined.
- The university has adopted a staff development policy and strategy, supported and reviewed at the highest level, which 'has delivered a much improved focus on the responsibilities and contributions of individuals, teams and the institution centrally towards the staff development process and the resources (the university applies) to it'.

- 'Communication and understanding on staff development issues, the importance of evaluating outcomes, and the relationship to business objectives have greatly improved at all levels throughout the university.'

The assessment

Following consideration of the university's written evidence, a three-person assessment team visited both university campuses during the week commencing 7 December 1998 and conducted one-to-one interviews with one lay member of Court and 98 staff who had been pre-selected as representative of the university's management, and its academic, research and support staff. Following these visits, the lead assessor presented his report to the Investors in People Recognition Panel and the university was formally recognized on 26 January 1999.

Continuing commitment

Following recognition, the University Principal, Professor Sir John Arbuthnott, wrote to all staff:

> I am delighted to advise that the university has been formally recognised as an Investor in People. This is a truly magnificent achievement in which we can all share pride and pleasure for the following reasons:
>
> - Strathclyde is the first of the pre-1992 research-based universities to have achieved the Standard.
> - The Standard could not have been achieved without the support and involvement of all our staff. The achievement enhances our reputation as a quality university, which is not afraid to innovate or to explain what it stands for in ways that will reach the widest possible audience.
> - To maintain the Standard the university will require to be reassessed. This ensures that the university's commitment to provide improved development opportunities for all its staff is a continuing one from which all staff can expect to benefit in the years ahead.

The university was successfully reviewed in March 2000. The findings of the assessor were overwhelmingly positive, noting that 'staff receive support from those in a position to offer such. . . and development needs in the wider context are considered'.

Case Study XII
BIKKER Communicatie BV

The organization

BIKKER is a communications agency based in the Netherlands. It was founded in 1989 as a one-person business. The company helps their clients improve their communication possibilities including: corporate communication and reputation management, internal communication, employer branding and employee communication, product branding and branding experience, policy communication and interactive management.

Over a 10-year period the company has established a leading position in the Dutch communications consultancy market because of its drive and passion for innovation. BIKKER currently employs 80 people and another 50 in a (now related) interactive media consultancy called Human-I.

Based on its experience and up-to-date knowledge, BIKKER serves its clients through three advice teams. Each is supported by specialist teams: Concept Development; Corporate Identity and Design, Creation and Production; Medi@ Relations and Monitoring; Text Creation and Media Management. They also have staffing in IT and Telecom, Human Talent, Finance and Control, plus secretarial and administrative support. The staff of Human Talent have their own director who is also one of the three members of the general executive team.

The mission

BIKKER's mission statement is: 'Innovation in communication'. The company strives to become the quality market leader and the most attractive communications consultancy to work with and to work for – 'To work at BIKKER contributes to a challenging existence, professional growth and personal development'.

Reasons for making the initial commitment

From the beginning, the founder of BIKKER has been fascinated by the processes of motivating and developing staff, not only on behalf of the company but also for the benefit of the clientele. BIKKER has tried to be innovative in its HR policies relating to employee benefits, recruitment and professional career development. For example, it was the first company to introduce a flexible and individualized benefits scheme. Around 1995 BIKKER managers began to develop their own vision on HR management. It was their belief that 'the growth of an individual will determine the growth of a company' and that any investment in an individual's growth would create a positive outcome for the company. For five years they worked on tools to support the implementation of such a vision in their company. This vision and the related tools are summarized under a new heading: Human Talent Management, which is also the name of the staff department.

In early 1999 BIKKER was informed through the Chamber of Commerce about the planned Investors in People pilot project run by the Ministry of Economic Affairs. BIKKER's interest was heightened because of the similarity between its vision and that of Investors in People. BIKKER's management contacted the Ministry of Economic Affairs asking to join the pilot project, and the company was accepted as one of 20 organizations selected from a wide field to participate.

The senior managers of BIKKER were both convinced and committed with regard to piloting Investors in People. Although they felt that they should be able to meet the Standard without 'breaking too many eggs' they thought that Investors in People would be: firstly, a good test for the organization to prove that they were innovative enough in the field of human resources; and a mirror that could show them effectively if they had any blind spots.

The pilot project

At the start of the project BIKKER was provided with a Dutch Investors in People trained consultancy, Alpha Omega Adviesgroep. A project group of four people was formed from the Employability and Human Talent element of BIKKER. They were responsible for describing the current policy of the company in relation to the Standard and to set into motion all additional actions required. As expected, the organization did not need major changes as much of the work had been developed and embedded throughout the previous years. There was already a well-documented system of appraisal; people already worked with development plans; business plans were available; the mission statement was already shared and understood by everybody; and most of all the philosophy was already embedded in the business and in people's minds. This did not mean that BIKKER took up things lightly. Although intrinsically committed, managers realized that an explicit commitment of the executive team was of paramount importance, not only to comply with the Standard but mainly because this would enable the project group to do their work properly and to work on the blind spots that they were likely to discover. This also prevented Investors in People becoming a mere cosmetic exercise.

It was therefore not surprising that BIKKER did not need a lot of support from its consultants. During the initial phase, while measuring the company's activities against the Standard, the project group needed external support to help explain what was actually meant by some of the indicators. Later on advice was only necessary to test the action plan in relation to the Standard and to make the correct preparations for the assessment.

However, in mid-1999 the work of the project group became more complicated. A refocusing of some of the work processes was necessary in the light of an international partnership – an event not uncommon in this line of business. This led to some employees being transferred to the similar sister company in the network: Human-I. The impact of this on the assessment and the evidence required was unclear for the project group. Since this was also a totally new issue within the pilot project in the Netherlands it was decided that it was an opportune time to ask for advice from a UK Investors in People adviser. The adviser was then able to support the project group in their preparations for the assessment.

Linking with company philosophy

So how did Investors in People link with BIKKER philosophy? BIKKER has a relatively young workforce. For both the company and their clients they see 'human talent management' and personal responsibility as a business solution in a restricted labour market. Here are some positive results of putting this company philosophy into practice:

- BIKKER is well known to young and inexperienced academics as a company that gives a lot of opportunity to discover and grow. In the past sometimes the personal development of academics became an issue itself; now there is more balance between development issues and business targets.
- The annual appraisal is called a 'growth conversation'. BIKKER states that it takes a lot of time to map the ambitions of all the individuals and match them with the business goals and opportunities. But the growth conversations (each conversation taking up an hour and a half or more) are very popular with all staff. One of the crucial appraisal dimensions is proof of successful growth.
- Each year, every member of staff has a budget up to the level of one month's salary to spend on his or her own growth. The growth conversation determines the goals on which to spend this money. Managers have the task of coaching their staff about the right way to make use of personal growth opportunities as money not spent on development cannot be carried forward.
- To support management and staff with training information there is information on the Intranet; each person is also encouraged to use the same database to share the evaluation of their training experiences.
- To support development and growth further BIKKER experimented last year with 360 degree feedback. Feedback from

management and staff from this experiment has been very positive. This tool is now in use annually for all staff.

- Human talent management and Investors in People is used by BIKKER as an explicit recruitment and selection issue; 'growth' being an offer as well as a demand. Managers and staff also use the same philosophy to manage issues like absence, sickness, work stress, etc.
- Each member of staff has a business card with his or her own personal motto making a statement about what values he or she believes in.
- The management of BIKKER as well as the staff are relatively young; some of them have limited management experience. Therefore to further improve and implement human talent management and Investors in People BIKKER are setting up a coaching system for their line managers.

The blindspots

Internal communications

Not all staff had the 'right' information at the right time. This problem emerged particularly during the period of investigating the international partnership and its consequences. The new management team created guidelines regarding their internal communication. At each weekly management meeting it is decided what issues should be communicated and when, how and why this should be done.

Evaluation

Evaluating the outcomes and the contents of training was – and still is – seen as an individual responsibility. Now, however, there is more attention to the beneficial effects of sharing these evaluations with the rest of the staff.

BIKKER was assessed for Investors in People status and subsequently recognized at the end of 1999.

The benefits

These include:

- Raising the involvement and commitment of staff.
- Raising enthusiasm, which has been noticed by the company's clients.
- Being able to offer 'state-of-the-art' advisers – seen by BIKKER as arguably the most important point.

Key messages

BIKKER suggests that other organizations working towards Investors in People status should start working on their own human talent philosophy and look for the tools they need rather than using Investors in People to do this for them. The same philosophy should be used throughout the whole business, for example, in recruitment and selection.

CHAPTER 11

Maintaining and Retaining Recognition

This chapter will be of potential interest and value to most readers as it introduces elements of what can happen following initial recognition. Recognized organizations will find more detail about retaining and developing Investors in People status in *Investors in People Maintained* (2001) by the same authors.

In this chapter the type, style and nature of feedback given to the organization by the assessor is described, as well as how the LLSC/LEC/T&EA maintain contact during the period between recognition and the date when reassessment is due. It also briefly introduces the concept of the 'post-recognition review' processes (formerly known as reassessment).

When should reassessment take place?

Recognition as an Investor in People was originally scheduled to last for a maximum of three years. Many organizations and practitioners questioned the logic behind the length of this period. This question has now been addressed by offering organizations increased flexibility and choice. Originally the idea was that recognition could last for a maximum of three years and it would be up to TECs/LECs to decide if they wanted to reassess within that period. Most TECs/LECs indicated at the time that they were likely to wait the full three-year period before reassessing. To maintain national consistency it was decided that there would be no optional time-frame and all recognitions should last for three years. The thinking at the time suggested that, at that stage of the development of the Standard, three years was an appropriate period of time. The reasons can be summarized as follows:

- Investors in People concerns strategic planning. It is possible that some organizations may not be able to demonstrate some of the significant improvements and benefits in less than that period.
- There was a commonly held view that organizations would understandably question the logic of having an assessment every year in terms of cost and added value.
- TECs were not able to cope with the resource implications of reassessing every year.

These reasons are still valid, but the introduction of the post-recognition review (outlined later in this chapter) has offered organizations more opportunities to make the process more in keeping with their planning cycle without sending costs through the roof.

The first reassessments

Following the first recognitions in 1991, TECs/LECs were encouraged to maintain contact with recognized organizations. This contact could be on an informal basis but a dialogue was encouraged that would indicate to the TEC whether the organization was continuing to demonstrate its commitment to being an Investor in People.

In practice, contact was maintained initially because the first organizations to be recognized were frequently invited to speak at events hosted by TECs and other interested organizations. However, evidence from the first reassessments indicates that the contact during the three-year period was not always as structured as had been planned and expected. Many organizations therefore were left unsupported and uninformed as to what the reassessment process would involve. It is inappropriate to apportion blame for this situation, although the Government at the time had set targets to be achieved over a period shorter than most informed sources thought appropriate. Attention was focused on increasing the number of organizations that were making the commitment to become Investors in People and on carrying out assessments of those that had completed the journey.

Three years seemed a long way off when recognition was first secured and the issue of reassessment was often set aside to be dealt with 'in due course' when 'more immediate priorities had been dealt with'. In addition, the turnover of TEC staff at this time was particularly high. This was especially true in the case of those staff who were seconded civil servants wishing to return to the service. This compounded the difficulty as they were replaced by staff who had much to learn and were under pressure to do so very quickly indeed.

Most of the organizations first assessed were given little, if any, feedback and therefore did not have an agreed agenda for the three-year period. Although attempts were made over the ensuing three-year period to offer guidance and support with regard to reassessment, it was evident that what was needed for the future was regular, structured contact *throughout* the three-year period.

As with any new process the skills and expertise of the people involved developed and, although the process that the first organizations experienced is more or less the same as the current one, the manner in which it is carried out has been refined considerably into a far more sophisticated and rigorous process. In other words, lessons have been learnt, assessors are now much more skilled, and the whole quality assurance process has been greatly enhanced.

Post-assessment feedback to organizations

The first significant lesson learnt from the early assessments underpinned the importance of offering feedback to organizations, following the decision by the Recognition Panel to recognize an organization.

One of the benefits of an external assessor examining the processes and systems within an organization is that they invariably discover that although processes and systems are working effectively, they can always be improved. This was further encouraged by Recognition Panels who were increasingly very suspicious of assessors' reports of organizations that appear 'too good'. Assessors were therefore encouraged to present a picture which was realistic and include issues that, although meeting the requirements of the standard, could be improved. Recognition Panels themselves also offered assessors a range of issues that they would like fed back to organizations.

Frequently the feedback concerned issues about evaluation. Although organizations may have demonstrated sufficient evidence to meet the requirements of the indicators, it was often clear to assessors that there were opportunities to have objectives, targets and standards that better focused, which would lead to improved evaluation.

Normally the feedback was given by the assessor with an adviser from the TEC/LEC present. The assessor then withdrew and the adviser discussed with the representative of the organization how these issues could be taken forward and whether the TEC/LEC could offer support.

In the spirit of *kaizen* (the search for a better way), most organizations welcomed this feedback. The feedback, in effect, set part of the agenda for the next three years (or sooner if an earlier review was chosen) and in reality started the reassessment process. Some TECs/LECs encouraged organizations to develop an action plan for the period between assessments/reviews.

Many TECs/LECs also encouraged organizations that had been recognized to continue networking to support one another throughout the three years.

The demise of the portfolio

The second major lesson learnt concerned the style and content of the portfolio. Portfolios became, in the main, much more streamlined and better presented but since the completion of the STAR project (see Chapter 1) they have become a rare occurrence at reviews. (As noted earlier, there is not – and never has been – a formal requirement for a portfolio, but a small number of organizations still find compiling one useful – even at reviews.)

Lessons learnt from the first reassessments

Lessons are still being learnt, of course, in the spirit of continuous improvement. However, as mentioned earlier, the process of reassessment for most organizations might well have been experienced quite differently. This may be in part due to the greatly enhanced professional development and experience of assessors. For example, the first assessments placed more emphasis on the portfolio of evidence than on the site visit and interviews. Almost immediately assessors placed more and more emphasis on the site visit and individual responses to the assessor. This came to be regarded as the 'acid test' as to whether an organization was actually an Investor in People.

TECs/LECs probably did not maintain sufficient structured contact, especially with the early recognized organizations, during the three-year period.

The excitement and enthusiasm generated by undertaking the journey and achieving recognition typically soon passed and things began to plateau. Systems can always atrophy, if care is not taken to review and modify them to keep them fresh and motivate people (especially line managers) to continue to use them. This happened with a number of organizations – and still can if appropriate internal measures are not taken.

In 1996 a specific indicator concerning continuous improvement was introduced. This encouraged many recognized organizations to be more aware of the need to review the effectiveness of processes as well as the effectiveness of the training and development itself. As indicated in Chapters 8, 9 and 10 the current Standard also encourages organizations to seek to continuously improve (indicator 12). Whilst the recent revisions to the Standard focus on outcomes they are underpinned by an expectation of processes (however the organization chooses to structure and present them). Therefore care should be taken to continue to evaluate the effectiveness of these processes – the 'so what?' question again!

Some organizations felt that the three-year reassessment model offered little added value. This view, though, was far from unanimous. Many organizations took stock prior to the reassessment process and this alerted them to the fact that, because of other priorities, they had lost the focus on recording and evaluating the development that had taken place. Clearly the discipline of being reassessed on a regular basis ensures that organizations do not, and will not, let things slide.

Continuing refinement of the reassessment process

After the first reassessments there was some dissatisfaction with the process. This triggered a debate about what the reassessment process should look like. A project was commissioned in 1995 to examine the issues around reassessment. From this a model emerged and was introduced, following testing via a series of pilots, in August 1998.

The results of the project showed that a key concern among many (but certainly not all) employers was the lack of TEC/LEC contact between assessments. Also of concern was that, in most cases, there was no funding to help organizations prepare for reassessment.

All the organizations that were involved in the project had undergone significant changes during the three-year period, so a major reassessment was invariably needed. The majority of organizations questioned the benefit – especially when faced with the costs of such a reassessment. Larger organizations were looking to develop an integrated management approach to quality and therefore were in favour of internalizing the assessment process and having some form of external verification.

Post-recognition review (the reassessment model)

From June 1998, following the completion of the research and pilots, once organizations had been recognized they were invited to choose which model they wanted to opt for, ie a three-year reassessment or a 12–15 month reassessment.

However, there was still an element of dissatisfaction with the restrictive nature of the 12–15 month period, so Investors in People UK decided that the constraint of the 12–15 month timescale would be removed. Since July 1999 organizations, immediately after being recognized for the first time, have been asked to choose when they wish to be reassessed. This can be at any time provided that it takes place at least once every three years. If they wish they can be assessed more than once within the three-year period. No matter how frequent, each review must cover the whole Standard.

The process

Although there are no national rules most units follow a similar process. One month prior to the chosen time for the review visit the organization is asked to provide the assessor with:

- information on a pro forma about organizational changes since the last assessment or review;
- information about the organization's plan setting out clear goals and targets and the organization's training and development needs
- an organization chart and/or staff list.

The assessor reviews this documentation along with the feedback or review report to determine the key issues for the review visit, which will be then agreed with the organization. Objectives will focus mainly on areas of the organization that have undergone change. The assessor's methodology will be based on following audit trails of issues/objectives and supporting processes.

The assessor makes an on-site judgement, identifies any development areas and feeds them back to senior managers before leaving the site. This is then followed up by a report. The number of changes that have taken place and the frequency of the review will clearly have an impact on the length and depth of the assessment.

If the assessor finds that the organization has not continued to meet all the indicators, the areas where the Standard has not been met will be identified by the assessor. The organization will be expected to develop a plan outlining the action to be taken to address these areas. This may, of course, be done in association with external advisers. The plan is expected to be produced within three months and the action to be completed within 12 months. In the meantime the organization will not lose its recognition as an Investor in People. However, if the organization does not wish to address the areas then recognition will be withdrawn.

Assessor–client relationships

Although initially there was a debate about whether the original assessor should be used for reassessments, in practice (until recently) most reassessments were undertaken by a different assessor, although the guidelines did not insist that this was the case. Indeed, most Assessment Units now favour the practice of looking for the same assessor to undertake the review. There are advantages in having the same assessor, particularly concerning the speed with which the assessor can assess progress. The danger is that the assessor may creep into an advisory role and a conflict of interest between advice and assessment may emerge. There are strong and compelling arguments drawn from experience that suggest a review by a 'critical friend' is more rigorous and cost effective.

Post-assessment feedback

Research conducted in 1998 by Investors in People UK showed that employers find the feedback meetings increasingly important and valuable. This is especially true where more frequent reassessments take place, and where the report forms the key elements of the agenda for the next visit. Clearly assessors need to continue to develop their ability to offer immediate constructive feedback following assessments. The added value of external assessment and reassessment will mainly be derived from this feedback.

Summary

This chapter has examined the options for reassessment, or as it is now known, the post-recognition review. It has outlined the rationale behind the development of the process. It has also highlighted the importance of feedback to the organization at the end of the process.

CHAPTER 12

Learning to be a Learning Organization

This chapter looks at how Investors in People can support the process of managing and achieving systemic organization-wide change by setting it in the wider context of what it means to be a learning organization. This chapter will be of particular interest to trainers and developers, students and managers with an interest in a corporate approach to enhancing individuals' contribution to continuous improvement.

As we have illustrated throughout this book, the Investors in People process offers support in improving and developing the individual, the unit and the organization in line with business objectives. As a vehicle promoting and supporting the management of change and an instrument designed to encourage empowerment of employees, Investors in People is potentially a very powerful process. The experience of organizations in our case studies confirms this.

What is a learning organization?

The concept of a learning organization developed out of the self-development movement from the 1970s onwards, which clearly stressed each individual person's responsibility for addressing his or her own training and career development needs. In many cases people experienced this very positively, but all too often inflexible organizational structures, entrenched centralist policies or lack of recognition by the organization itself of employees' self-development actions acted as real barriers to self-development in practice.

Gradually it was suggested that it was organizations that needed to be open to, and value, learning for themselves as total entities: learning for organizations as well as learning for individuals in organizations. This idea was encapsulated in the learning organization literature from the late 1980s and is clearly of increasing use and value for the 1990s as Investors in People continues to attract more and more organizations. There are a number of views as to what exactly a learning organization is. Some of these are summarized below for the interested reader, others can skip to the section that summarizes the main characteristics.

Definitions

John Burgoyne (1992) has offered the following working definition of a learning organization: 'A learning organization continuously transforms itself in the process reciprocally linked to the development of all its members.' Alternatively Mills and Friesen (1992) have described it as follows:

> We conceive of a learning organization as one able to sustain consistent innovation or 'learning', with the immediate goals of improving quality, enhancing customer or supplier relationships, more effectively executing business strategy, and the ultimate objective of sustaining profitability.

Other definitions include 'A learning organisation is one that is continually expanding its capacity to create its future.' (Senge, 1990) and 'A learning organisation harnesses the full brainpower, knowledge and experience available to it, in order to evolve continually for the benefit of all its stakeholders.' (Mayo and Lank, 1994).

We would define learning organizations as those organizations that link *understanding* the benefits of developing their people with *improving the quality* of what they do and/or produce. This improves their relationship with their key stakeholders (both internal and external), increases efficiency and effectiveness, and –

most importantly – enables them to stay in existence. This, we believe, entitles them to consider themselves as learning to be learning organizations whether or not they articulate it as such!

Peter Senge has been something of a guru on this topic. He describes five 'disciplines' of a learning organization as follows:

- personal mastery – continuous learning by the individual;
- mental models – examining the way in which we view the world;
- building a shared vision – something that pulls everyone towards a common long-term goal;
- team learning – thinking together and producing results better than the members would on their own;
- systems thinking – seeing the relationships between all the components of the organization.

(Senge,1994).

Main characteristics of a learning organization

Based on research from a number of organizations, some 11 characteristics have been identified which describe learning organizations in practical terms:

- *A learning approach to strategy or policy*, whereby the very way an organization decides collectively what to do and how to implement it, with ongoing monitoring and review, and adaptation of plans along the way, is itself a learning process.
- *Participative policy-making*, which involves as many people as possible in the policy-making process, resulting in better local implementation and greater commitment and ownership of the plan or plans, or as Burgoyne states (1992), 'This may take much longer than it might when policy is decided by a small private group of people but what you lose in the extra discussion and thinking time you get back in the implementation time.'
- *Informing*, using open information systems to make key information available as widely as possible throughout the organization, which supports participative policy-making

(above) but also provides the foundation for all the other characteristics.

- *Formative accounting and control*, the provision of up-to-date information about the potential consequences of various actions in order to assist in local decision-making and in making changes in a more timely way.
- *Mutual adjustment between departments*, the importance of each department or part of an organization viewing itself as a customer of, or supplier to, another department or unit (emanating from a TQM philosophy) and proactively working alongside one another rather than only to top–down control.
- *Reward flexibility*, having available within organizations the right kind of rewards and conditions for individuals in ways that reinforce learning.
- *Adaptable structures*, possessing the ability to change structures and procedures relatively easily and cheaply.
- *Boundary workers as environmental scanners*, the ability of organizations to learn about their environments from their own people, particularly those who interact directly with the customer at the internal (departmental) and external (client interface) boundaries.
- *Inter-organizational learning*, the encouragement of everyone in the whole organization to learn from everyone else, including internal and external suppliers.
- *A particular kind of culture and climate*, a climate that promotes learning, including positive learning from mistakes: 'It's all right to make a mistake once but it is not all right to make the same mistake two or three times' and a leadership style that encourages taking some responsible risks but offers support and two-way communication throughout.
- *Self-development opportunities for all*, whereby people have some degree of self-management and self-control over their own development and career progression, but which is guided, facilitated and resourced by the organization.

The case studies in Part Three describe how some of these characteristics and the principles underlying the Investors in People initiative were realized in practice.

Benchmarking the learning organization

We believe that subscribing to the Investors in People process demands the creation of a learning organization. The organizations featured in our case studies in Part Three demonstrated in practice the value of investing in people. They all exhibit many of the characteristics of a learning organization. Most have:

- a culture that values and rewards learning;
- personal and professional development integrated into strategic planning;
- systems and specialists that are used to enhance personal and professional development;
- clear development and support offered equally to all staff throughout their time with the organization and at all stages of their career;
- a clear and well-articulated link between development and appraisal;
- evaluation as an integral part of the personal and professional development iterative loop.

The potential of Investors in People is rooted, as we have noted, in its training and development orientation. Most organizations are engaged in the provision of the training and professional development of existing and future employees, and many may well have already acquired either a TQM award or a quality assurance standard such as ISO 9000. It might well be perceived as advantageous by their present and potential customers for them to pursue Investors in People.

The other significant tenet of Investors in People is its direct link with business objectives. It has to be hoped that the development of clear objectives for the organization and its constituent units, and the process of explaining these objectives to all staff, will engender that essential sense of ownership via an understanding of what needs to be achieved and what every individual's contribution is.

Recent developments

John Burgoyne, writing in *People Management* (June 1999) argues that we have 'the conditions in which a second generation of learning organisation can be developed'. This requires the concept of continuous learning to become a reality and Burgoyne lists the main factors needed in making this happen:

- Companies must become more aware of the internal politics they need to tackle.
- Managers ought to be clearer about where the collective learning process takes place and where the consequent knowledge is located.
- Strategies to share learning are required to enable collective learning to occur in the fragmented and loosely coupled forms taken by many organizations.
- Learning organizations need to create their own organizational development 'tools'.
- The issues of achieving synergy among stakeholders must be dealt with.
- More safeguards are needed to prevent misuse.
- Organizations have to deal clearly with the issue of ownership of competence and intellectual property between the employee and the organization.
- Processes and strategies are required to deal with the interaction between tacit and explicit knowledge.
- We must work out how the use of language can both help organizational learning and hinder it.
- The learning organization requires systems to ensure that its own ideas and processes can be challenged and reviewed.

Summary

This chapter has sought to describe the main features of a learning organization and to demonstrate that the Investors in People Standard cannot be achieved without clear evidence of commitment at the highest level. The managing director or chief executive will be formally interviewed by the assessor and the response will be set against other (formal and informal) interviews or conversations that the assessor will have had over the final formal assessment period. Recognition will not be gained unless a clear corporate approach is reflected by a critical proportion of the staff.

The central theme of this chapter is, therefore, that the Investors in People process is most certainly not merely concerned with training but also about practically adding value to an organization's existing and future assets. It is more than a mere paper exercise and it is not a bureaucratic straitjacket. On the contrary, it offers a positive process in support of change management that is essentially qualitative, whatever the organizational focus might be.

CHAPTER 13

Sources of Help

This chapter is a 'Who's Who' of the various sources of help available to organizations who want to gain or retain Investors in People status. As addresses and telephone numbers can soon become out of date it does not give full details of all the sources. It does not attempt to list all sources but merely points to the key players who in turn may have their own sources to which they redirect anyone who wants to know more.

Investors in People UK

Investors in People UK was established in July 1993 as a private company limited by guarantee. It opened for business on 1 October 1993. Originally based in Sheffield, it moved to premises at 7–10 Chandos Street, London W1G 9DQ in April 1994. Investors in People has a Web site: http://www.investorsinpeople.co.uk/

The role of Investors in People UK is:

- to guard, direct and take the lead on the development of the Investors in People National Standard, in the UK and internationally;
- to define the assessment process in outline;
- to handle national promotion and support;
- to provide a national quality assurance service;

- to assess and award recognition to national organizations and originally TECs/LECs and now local Learning and Skills Councils;
- to promote the Standard internationally.

Investors in People UK works in close consultation with all its partners.

Investors in People UK and SMS software (see software below) offer complementary products at a similar price that are adaptable to the needs of most organizations and sectors. Both products are designed to assist those responsible for managing their organization's progress through the Investors in People process. The Investors in People Software offered by Investors in People UK brings together the whole process of achieving and maintaining Standard. It is designed to allow the user to self assess their position, accurately, against each indicator, identify the gaps, create an action plan and prepare for assessment. The software includes survey materials and has a feature that allows different parts of an organization to be compared. The software is available from Investors in People UK with a licence for the software costing £180 inclusive of VAT. Licences for additional computers in the same organization cost £50 inclusive of VAT.

National Training Organizations (NTOs)

NTO National Council was founded in October 1997 to represent and support the new network of National Training Organisations (NTOs) that was launched in May 1998. Its predecessor organization, NCITO, represented Industry Training Organisations (ITOs) and other related bodies from the 1980s.

The launch of the NTO network marked a major rationalization of the previous infrastructure, replacing the ITOs, Lead Bodies and Occupational Standards Councils (OSCs) that had been in existence from the 1980s, with a single NTO for each industry or occupational sector. In addition to taking over many of these organizations' activities, NTOs have a far wider strategic remit defined by government.

Every business sector has its own NTO. The number of NTOs recognized by the Government to date is 75, each representing an individual industry (such as construction or hospitality), or occupation that affects all sectors (such as information technology or management). NTOs cover the whole of the UK. They are owned and supported by employers and serve organizations of every size.

NTOs' role is to bring together employers, Government and the world of education and training to define and take forward a focused agenda for skills. Their work ranges from assisting in the development and implementation of national and regional policies on learning and skills, to assessing the skills needs and impact of their sector and developing practical solutions to training problems on behalf of their industries. NTOs have a key role with regard to Investors in People – for example joint projects, producing practical guides, case studies and other supportive sector-specific material.

NTOs' origins date back to the mid-1960s, when the Government made the first moves towards a structure of employer representation. A network of Industry Training Boards (ITBs) was established. ITBs were given the power to raise a levy to be used to further vocational education and training from companies within their defined sectors.

During the 1980s most ITBs were wound-up and ITOs were developed. By the mid-1990s – and with the expansion of the NVQ/SVQ system – the plethora of organizations, ie ITOs, Lead Bodies, and OSCs had become extremely confusing for business people. All existing ITOs, Lead Bodies and OSCs were provided with a detailed prospectus containing new criteria and were invited to apply for recognition as NTOs.

One of the authors works for the NTO for Higher Education (HESDA, see below). Their first aim is 'to promote strategically planned, continuing and coherent staff development and training provision across universities and colleges in the United Kingdom'.

For further information about NTOs contact, The NTO National Council, 10 Amos Road, Meadow Court, Sheffield S9 1BX (tel: 0114 261 9926). Web site: http://www.nto-nc.org

Learning and Skills Councils and TECs

The Learning and Skills Council (LSC) and the network of local Learning and Skills Councils (LLSC) will be operational from April 2001. Their role is to fund further education and take forward government funded training and workforce development in England with a budget of some £5 billion. The LLSCs are planned to succeed the Training and Enterprise Councils (TECs) which in 2000 was spending £1 billion on training and the Further Education Funding

Council which was spending over £3 billion on further education. The enterprise role of TECs is to be taken forward by the DTI's Small Business Service.

Raising standards and delivering high quality training, including national learning targets, will be central to the success of the LSC which will also include a new inspection system, based on existing expertise with work-based training, to help drive up quality. Information about the LSC and the LLSCs can be found on the DfEE Web site: www.dfee.gov.uk/post16/

Information about the Small Business Service can be found on: www.businessadviceonline.org

The Higher Education' Staff Development Agency (HESDA)

HESDA, formerly known as UCoSDA was created in 1989. It is one of the agencies of the Committee of Vice Chancellors and Principals and was recognized as the NTO for higher education (THETO) in November 1997.

HESDA seeks to provide advice, support and resources to its member universities and colleges in the planning, organization, provision and evaluation of continuing professional/vocational development for all personnel in the higher education sector.

It currently employs an approved Investors in People assessor – one of the authors of this book. The HESDA philosophy captures some of the central themes of this book and is summarized as follows:

Investment in the personal, professional and vocational development of all staff employed by universities and colleges is fundamental:

(a) to the successful achievement of organizational goals and
(b) to the motivation and continuing capacity of individual staff members to support that achievement.

HESDA has produced a number of briefing papers and other publications on Investors in People and related issues and can be contacted at the following address: Ingram House, 65 Wilkinson Street, The University of Sheffield, Sheffield S10 2GJ (tel: 0114 282 4211; fax: 0114 272 8705). Web site: www.hesda.org.uk

Scotland – Local Enterprise Companies (LECs)

LECs were set up at about the same time as TECs but they have a wider remit than TECs as they not only took over the delivery of products and services such as Youth and Adult Training but also embraced the role of the Scottish Development Agency and the Highlands and Islands Development Agency.

The 22 LECs are private companies limited by guarantee who are contracted to either Scottish Enterprise or Highlands and Islands Enterprise. Assessment and recognition is carried out by Investors in People Scotland, so the role of the LECs is to carry out the same work as TECs minus assessment and recognition. They too use outsiders to deliver various stages of Investors in People.

The telephone numbers and addresses of LECs can be found in local telephone directories.

Investors in People Scotland

The role of Investors in People Scotland has been described in Chapter 6.

Northern Ireland – Training and Employment Agency (T&EA)

The T&EA was established as an agency of the Northern Ireland Civil Service in 1990 and is now part of the Department of Higher and Further Education, Training and Employment. It carries out a role similar to that of the DfEE in Britain.

One of its divisions has a particular remit to support business and it is under this requirement that Investors in People sits.

The Agency has broadly the same role as the TECs in delivering Investors in People. However, the financial support offered by the T&EA is through the Agency's Company Development Programme and the consultants who deliver it.

Management and Enterprise Training Organisation (METO)/Management Charter Initiative (MCI)

For information on the MCI Management Standards or the booklets *Managing Business Success* and *The Good Managers Guide* contact METO at the following address: Russell Square House, 10–12 Russell Square, London WC1B 5BZ (tel: 020 7872 9000).

MCI and the Small Firms Enterprise Development Initiative formed an alliance to establish the Management and Enterprise Training Organization. Launched in July 1998, it is the NTO for management and enterprise. As well as its responsibility for management and the management standards it has additional responsibilities for design, marketing, sales, supply chain management and international trade. It draws together these elements in a coordinated approach to education, research, training and development to increase Britain's competitiveness.

MCI's Web site is: www.management-charter-initiative.org.uk

Consultants and consultancy organizations

Feelings about using consultants differ considerably from one organization (or person) to another. This section does not intend to debate the relative merits of using consultants; the arguments are well rehearsed elsewhere. However, because the resources within TECs have been limited, they and LECs have encouraged the use of outside help to deliver the various stages of Investors in People. As in-house expertise grew, and budgets were reduced, some TECs in particular used their own staff to offer assistance. The changes to the assessment process also led to less reliance on consultants, particularly for smaller organizations. With the advent of LSCs and the Small Business Service we will have to wait and see if there is sufficient in-house resource or whether there may be a resurgence in demand for help from external sources.

Investors in People UK developed a quality assurance process for consultants and advisers who work with organizations on Investors in People. The process covers roles such as selling, diagnosing and developing and implementing action plans and is managed by a number of Advisory Registration Units (ARUs) throughout the UK and approved by Investors in People UK. At the moment the quality assurance registration process for potential advisers involves sitting a written multi-choice examination followed by a situational interview in front of an interview panel.

Investors in People UK took an interest in this subject as the credibility of the process of becoming an Investor in People was being affected because advice and guidance being given was not as good as it should have been. Although the process for consultants and advisors new to Investors in People will change from Apr 2001 there will still be a quality assurance process which will us the new Investors in People practitioner competences as a basis plu an interview.

How consultants can help

Provided you get the right consultant he or she can help in a numbe of ways. Consultants may help you secure some financial suppor They should have experience of carrying out certain tasks and ca therefore help you avoid reinventing wheels.

They *should* know what is expected of you by an assessor bu ensure that you are not merely introducing things for an assesso but are doing them for sound business reasons too. In most case the needs of the assessor will coincide with your needs but yo need to challenge the consultant constantly if you feel you are bein asked to do something from which you will gain no busines benefits.

Consultants should have experience or an understanding o related models ISO 9000, the Excellence Model, OFSTED, Lexce and other quality models and processes and how they complemen Investors in People. Again this will avoid re-inventing wheels.

When consultants can help

Consultants can help with:

- initial diagnosis and action planning (but see Chapter 4);
- advice and guidance with implementation of plans;
- assessment.

Other organizations

The help offered by peers who are going through the process wa mentioned earlier, but what about those organizations that hav already been recognized? The first organizations to be recognize were inundated by callers who wanted to know how they did i some of them may well have wondered why they got involved. How ever, there are now a lot more people to offer this kind of guidanc

Most LLSC/TECs and LECs invite representatives from recog nized organizations to speak at local events, so you may well fin out about them then. If not, or if you need to identify a specifi type of organization, your LLSC/TEC or LEC should be able to put you in touch with someone who can help.

Software

A wide range of software has been designed to help and support organizations to gain and maintain Investors in People status.

SMS software have developed a particularly useful product that is adaptable to the needs of most organizations and sectors called 'Investors in People Manager'. It is a PC software package designed to assist those responsible for managing their organization's progress through the Investors in People process. By examining each evidence requirement in turn it helps you build up the necessary action plan and then use its project management tools to achieve the desired outcomes. It also includes a wide range of useful tips and examples with full reporting facilities. The package ably supports the project management process at all levels.

Amongst the users of the software were AstraZeneca, Maccles-field Site, formally Zeneca Pharmaceuticals, who were first accredited as an Investor In People in 1994, and in January 2000 successfully gained its second re-accreditation.

AstraZeneca commented as follows:

> In order to simplify referencing of data and tracking progress against the indicators it was decided to use SMS software.
>
> The software was mainly used for referencing evidence against the indicators and providing an evidence matrix. Throughout the preparation the software provided ... (the) simple approach (of) changing data and instantly seeing the consequences of new data on the reports that could be produced.
>
> The final portfolio produced prior to the assessment consisted of two files, one Investors in People reference data including SMS reports and a second consisting of one example per indicator. The result being professional documents which supported the successful re-accreditation process.

In association with the publishers of this book, Kogan Page, SMS are pleased to be able to offer readers a discount on the purchase of this software (normal price £200.00 + VAT). To take advantage of this offer telephone SMS on 0151 227 2393 and they will supply the software for £185.00 + VAT.

Overseas sources of help

Sources of help overseas is a little more complex. Investors in People UK have developed strategic partnerships to pilot Investors in People. In the first overseas country to launch Australia, for example the strategic Partner is NCSI (Nata Certification Services International), an existing organization. In Finland the partner is the University of Helsinki whilst in the Netherlands a new body has been established – Investors in People Nederland.

At the same time consultancies who can assist organizations are emerging as sources of advice, such as the PerSyst ECPM Consultancy in the Netherlands who found the BIKKER case study for us (www.persyst-ecpm.com)

Visit the Investors in People UK Web site (see above) to discover who the strategic partner for each country is.

Various Investors in People material

Finally, there is a wealth of material available to help those working through the Investors in People process. Most TECs have produced their own material but in addition there is a lot of nationally available material produced by Investors in People UK (a catalogue is available and accessible via the Investors in People UK Web site – see above). There are also a lot of articles in management and training magazines and books to help you gain an understanding of what Investors in People is and how it can promote organizational development – (this book is an example!).

Appendix 1
The Investors in People Standard

Principles	Indicators	Evidence
Commitment An Investor in People is fully committed to developing its people in order to achieve its aims and objectives.	1 The organization is committed to supporting the development of its people.	Top management can **describe** strategies that they have put in place to support the development of people in order to improve the organization's performance. Managers can describe specific actions that they have taken and are currently taking to support the development of people. People can confirm that the specific strategies and actions described by top management and managers take place. People believe the organization is genuinely committed to supporting their development.
	2 People are encouraged to improve their own and other people's performance.	People can give examples of how they have been encouraged to improve their own performance.

Principles	Indicators	Evidence
	3 People believe their contribution to the organization is recognized.	People can describe how their contribution to the organization is recognized. People receive appropriate and constructive feedback on a timely and regular basis
	4 The organization is committed to ensuring equality of opportunity in the development of its people.	Top management can describe strategies that they have put in place to ensure equality of opportunity in the development of people. Managers can describe specific actions that they have taken and are currently taking to ensure equality of opportunity in the development of people. People confirm that the specific strategies and actions described by top management and managers take place and recognize the needs of different groups. People believe the organization is genuinely committed to ensuring equality of opportunity in the development of people.
Planning An Investor in People is clear about its aims and its objectives and what its people need to do to achieve them.	**5** The organization has a plan with clear aims and objectives which are understood by everyone.	The organization has a plan with clear aims and objectives. People can consistently explain the aims and objectives of the organization at a level appropriate to their role. Representative groups are consulted about the organization's aims and objectives.
	6 The development of people is in line with the organization's aims and objectives.	The organization has clear priorities which link the development of people to its aims and objectives at organization, team and individual level. People clearly understand what their development activities should achieve, both for them and the organization.

Principles	Indicators	Evidence
	7 People understand how they contribute to achieving the organization's aims and objectives.	People can explain how they contribute to achieving the organization's aims and objectives.
Action An Investor in People develops its people effectively in order to improve its performance.	8 Managers are effective in supporting the development of people.	The organization makes sure that managers have the knowledge and skills they need to develop their people. Managers at all levels understand what they need to do to support the development of people. People understand what their manager should be doing to support their development. Managers at all levels can give examples of actions that they have taken and are currently taking to support the development of people. People can describe how their managers are effective in supporting their development.
	9 People learn and develop effectively.	People who are new to the organization, and those new to a job, can confirm that they have received an effective induction. The organization can show that people learn and develop effectively. People understand why they have undertaken development activities and what they are expected to do as a result. People can give examples of what they have learnt (knowledge, skills and attitude) from development activities. Development is linked to relevant external qualifications or standards (or both), where appropriate.

Principles	Indicators	Evidence
Evaluation An Investor in People understands the impact of its investment in people on its performance.	**10** The development of people improves the performance of the organization, teams and individuals.	The organization can show that the development of people has improved the performance of the organization, teams and individuals.
	11 People understand the impact of the development of people on the performance of the organization, teams and individuals.	Top management understands the overall costs and benefits of the development of people and its impact on performance. People can explain the impact of their development on their performance, and the performance of their team and the organization as a whole.
	12 The organization gets better at developing its people.	People can give examples of relevant and timely improvements that have been made to development activities.

The Standard © Investors in People UK.

Appendix 2
Investors in People:
Senior Manager's Survey

Please tick the most relevant of the boxes on the right.

	Yes	No	Unsure
1. Is the organization committed to training and developing its people?	☐	☐	☐
2. Does the organization have a clear vision of how it will develop?	☐	☐	☐
3. If yes, has it been communicated to all employees?	☐	☐	☐
4. Does the organization have a business (or operational) plan with clear aims and objectives?	☐	☐	☐
5. Does the organization have a strategy to develop people in order to improve the organization?	☐	☐	☐
6. Could you describe the strategy?	☐	☐	☐
7. Does the strategy ensure equality of opportunity for development for all employees?	☐	☐	☐
8. Does the organization have clear priorities which link the development of people to its aims and objectives?	☐	☐	☐
9. If yes, have they been communicated to all employees?	☐	☐	☐

		Yes	No	Unsure
10.	Are all employees clear how their role contributes to helping the organization meet its business plan?	☐	☐	☐
11.	Has the organization ensured that managers have the knowledge and skills they need to develop their people?	☐	☐	☐
12.	Do they understand what they need to do to develop their people?	☐	☐	☐
13.	Do all people understand what their manager should do to develop their people?	☐	☐	☐
14.	Does the organization actively encourage and support all your employees in developing their skills?	☐	☐	☐
15.	Could you describe what you do to encourage and support your direct reports to develop their skills and knowledge?	☐	☐	☐
16.	Could you describe what you do to recognize the contribution that people make to the success of the organization?	☐	☐	☐
17.	Could the organization show that people learn and develop effectively?	☐	☐	☐
18.	Could the organization show that the development of people has improved the performance of:			
	a) the organization	☐	☐	☐
	b) the team	☐	☐	☐
	c) the individual?	☐	☐	☐
19.	Could you describe the costs and benefits of development activities?	☐	☐	☐

Appendix 3
Investors in People: Manager's Survey

Please tick the most relevant of the boxes on the right.

	Yes	No	Unsure
1. Is the organization committed to training and developing its people?	☐	☐	☐
2. Does the organization have a clear vision of how it will develop?	☐	☐	☐
3. If yes, has it been communicated to your team?	☐	☐	☐
4. Does the organization have a business (or operational) plan with clear aims and objectives?	☐	☐	☐
5. Does the organization have a strategy to develop people in order to improve the organization?	☐	☐	☐
6. Could you and your team describe the strategy?	☐	☐	☐
7. Does the strategy ensure equality of opportunity for development for all employees?	☐	☐	☐
8. Does the organization have clear priorities which link the development of people to its aims and objectives?	☐	☐	☐

		Yes	*No*	*Unsure*
9.	If yes, could you and your team describe the strategy?	☐	☐	☐
10.	Are all your team members clear how their role contributes to helping the organization meet its business plan?	☐	☐	☐
11.	Has the organization ensured that managers have the knowledge and skills they need to develop their people?	☐	☐	☐
12.	Do you understand what they need to do to develop their people?	☐	☐	☐
13.	Does your team understand what you should do to develop them?	☐	☐	☐
14.	Does the organization actively encourage and support you and your team to develop skills?	☐	☐	☐
15.	Could you describe what you do to encourage and support your team to develop their skills and knowledge?	☐	☐	☐
16.	Could you describe what you do to recognize the contribution that your people make to the success of the organization and your team?	☐	☐	☐
17.	Could you and your team give examples of what you have learnt?	☐	☐	☐
18.	Could you and your team describe examples that show the impact of the development of people on the performance of:			
	a) the organization	☐	☐	☐
	b) the team	☐	☐	☐
	c) the individual?	☐	☐	☐
19.	Could you and your team describe examples of improvements that have been made to development activities?	☐	☐	☐

Appendix 4
Investors in People: Employee's Survey

Please read each question carefully, then tick one of the boxes on the right. If you feel the question does not apply or that you do not know the answer you should tick the third box.

	Yes	*No*	*Unsure*
1. Could you describe what the organization does to support the development of people to improve its performance?	☐	☐	☐
2. If yes, do you believe that the actions meet the development needs of different groups of employees and promotes equality of opportunity for development?	☐	☐	☐
3. Could you give examples of how you have been encouraged to improve your own performance?	☐	☐	☐
4. Could you give examples of how you have been encouraged to improve other people's performance?	☐	☐	☐
5. Do you feel your contribution to the organization is recognized?	☐	☐	☐
If yes, could you describe how?	☐	☐	☐
6. Do you receive appropriate and constructive feedback on a regular basis?	☐	☐	☐

		Yes	*No*	*Unsure*
7.	Can you, in your own words, explain what the organization is trying to achieve?	☐	☐	☐
8.	Could you explain how your role helps the organization to meet its aims and objectives?	☐	☐	☐
9.	Could you describe what your manager should be doing to support your development?	☐	☐	☐
10.	Do you think your manager is effective in supporting your development?	☐	☐	☐
11.	If you started within the last 12 months, did you receive an effective induction?	☐	☐	☐
12.	When you undertook development activities were you always clear what you were expected to do as a result?	☐	☐	☐
13.	Could you give examples of what you have learnt from development activities in terms of knowledge and skills?	☐	☐	☐
14.	Could you explain what difference the development had on:			
	a) your performance	☐	☐	☐
	b) the performance of your team and	☐	☐	☐
	c) the organization as a whole?	☐	☐	☐
15.	Could you give examples of improvements that have been made to development activities within the organization?	☐	☐	☐
16.	Do you believe the organization is committed to developing its people?	☐	☐	☐

Appendix 5
Sample Size Guidelines

Number of staff employed	Sample band (%)
0–5	100
6–15	100–60
16–25	70–40
26–50	60–30
51–75	50–25
76–100	40–20
101–125	30–15
126–500	20–10
501–1,000	15–5
1,001–2,500	8–4
2,501–5,000	4–2
5,000+	3–1

Assessors should use their judgement when using the guidance above and bear in mind that, for example, where the number of staff is 76 it does not automatically require a sample of 40 per cent; it may require 20 per cent, depending on circumstances.

Source: Investors in People UK.

References

Burgoyne, J (1992) Creating a Learning Organisation, *RSA Journal*, **140**, pp 321–36, (April)

Burgoyne, J (1999) *People Management*, IPD

Handy, Constable and McCormack (1987) *The Making of British Managers*, British Institute of Management

Management Charter Initiative (MCI) (1998) *Managing Business Success*, MCI

MCI (1999) *The Good Managers Guide*, 2nd edn, MCI

Mayo, A and Lank, E (1994) *The Power of Learning: A Guide to Learning Independantly*, Open University Press

Mills, D Q and Friesen, B (1992) The Learning Organization, *European Managment Journal*, **10**, **2**, pp 146–56 (June)

Senge, P (1990) *The Fifth Discipline: The Art and Practice of the Learning Organization*, Doubleday

Taylor, P and Thackwray B (2001) *Investors in People – Maintained*, 2nd edn, Kogan Page, London

Taylor, P and Thackwray, B (2001) *Managing for Investors in People*, 2nd edn, Kogan Page, London

Training Agency, Department of Employment (1987) *Training in Britain*, DfEE, London

Vocational Education and Training Task Forces (1990) *Towards a Skill Revolution*, CBI, London

Index

References in *italic* indicate figures

203